Praise for *Delivering the Visitor Experience*

'After reading this book, I immediately w
my career. This is an absolute blueprint for anyone wanting to work in our incredible industry, from actually working in visitor experience to working alongside it and to understanding it better. It has made me remember why I first got into this industry as a duty manager and fell in love with that crucial role and the massive impact it has on everything in the museum.

I have worked in this industry for over 25 years yet still found myself writing notes whilst reading Rachel's book, from revisiting our Visitor Experience strategy, creating a shadow management team, to asking if the toilets should be more entertaining and how can I re-create *innri hringur* at the Mary Rose Museum?

On completion of her book, I thought every museum needs a Rachel Mackay working for it, but if that is not possible then getting this book is the next best alternative.

Rachel Mackay doesn't just give everyone involved in visitor experience a voice, she gives us a toolkit on how to do our jobs better.'
Dominic Jones, Chief Executive Officer, Mary Rose Trust

'Rachel Mackay's book *Delivering the Visitor Experience* is a comprehensive resource to consider how to create, develop, enrich or evolve the delivery of every aspect of a visitor's time within a cultural venue. If you care about your attraction, your staff and your visitors, this book is for you.

Mackay's voice and humour peppers the book taking it from a 'how-to' guide to a fun A–Z on creating and considering everything that impacts a customer during their visit. The book features tables and charts to assist understanding, and draws on case studies from multiple attractions to illustrate best practice.

I have read other publications around the subject, but Mackay's book feels fresh, authentic and accessible. Even the most seasoned Visitor Experience professional would take something from this book.'
Yvonne Honeyball, Visitor Experience and Operations Manager, Tate Britain

'This is an invaluable resource for anyone working within the much misunderstood and frequently overlooked area that is visitor experience. Rachel takes this vital frontline element of museum and heritage management and describes how to get it right, because getting it wrong is potentially disastrous. There are advocacy tips and helpful practical examples, such as how to make training sessions lively and entertaining, supporting staff working with challenging topics and crisis management planning. Rachel uses her knowledge and extensive industry contacts to outline a step-by-step approach to building a robust strategy and maintaining motivated, diverse teams committed to providing excellent visitor experiences. Importantly, case studies from across the world show how excellence and resilience can be achieved without placing stress on already stretched resources. This book is a must-read for any Visitor Experience professional.'

Sandra Lynes Timbrell, Director of Visitor Engagement, St Paul's Cathedral

Delivering the Visitor Experience

Museum and Gallery Essentials

Series Editors:
Maria Blyzinsky, Heritage Consultant and co-Founder of The Exhibitions Team
Rhiannon Goddard, Head of Public Engagement Projects and Business Management, Historic Royal Palaces

Today's museum and cultural heritage professionals are multi-taskers, under pressure to operate efficiently and effectively in the face of many competing demands. There are rarely enough hours in the day to prepare well for critical tasks and meetings. Taking time out to think things through and plan properly can sometimes be seen as a luxury, which can lead to feeling overwhelmed by the tasks ahead. In addition, today's fast-paced world can throw up unforeseen challenges – such as the lockdowns of the COVID-19 pandemic or economic downturns. We may not be able to predict every challenge, but we can develop creative and critical thinking to help with problem-solving.

Museum and Gallery Essentials taps into the expertise of established professionals from across the sector. The series provides guidance that supports practitioners managing today's complex situations and challenges while also providing students with the frameworks and knowledge needed at the start of their careers. Each guide is carefully crafted to provide a highly practical road map, helping readers to think effectively, creatively and strategically when solving issues under pressure and with limited resources.

The Editors welcome proposals from cultural heritage professionals across a range of topics, including approaches to decolonisation, tackling the climate emergency, interpretation, collections management and care, registration, learning and outreach, financial management and curatorship. For more information, please contact info@facetpublishing.co.uk.

Delivering the Visitor Experience

How to Create, Manage and Develop an Unforgettable Visitor Experience at Your Museum

Rachel Mackay

facet publishing

Published by Facet Publishing
c/o British Library, 96 Euston Road, London NW1 2DB
www.facetpublishing.co.uk

Facet Publishing is wholly owned by CILIP: the Library and Information Association.

British Library Cataloguing in Publication Data
A catalogue record for this book is available from the British Library.

ISBN 978-1-78330-549-0 (paperback)
ISBN 978-1-78330-550-6 (hardback)
ISBN 978-1-78330-551-3 (PDF)
ISBN 978-1-78330-552-0 (EPUB)

First published 2023

MIX
Paper | Supporting responsible forestry
FSC® C013604

Every purchase of a Facet book helps to fund CILIP's advocacy awareness and accreditation programmes for information professionals.

Typeset from author's files by Flagholme Publishing Services in 10/13 pt Palatino Linotype and Open Sans.
Printed and made in Great Britain by CPI Group (UK) Ltd, Croydon, CR0 4YY.

Contents

Figures, Tables and Case Studies

Figures

Tables

Case Studies

About the Author

Rachel Mackay was born in Dundee, Scotland. Since the age of 16 she has been working in visitor-focused roles in the museum and heritage sector. Starting out in museum cafés at Verdant Works: Scotland's Jute Museum and Dundee Science Centre, Rachel moved to London in 2009 and carved out a career developing and delivering the visitor experience in roles at Madame Tussauds, the Natural History Museum and Kew Palace.

As a consultant, Rachel has advised on Visitor Experience projects at the Jewish Museum London, Chelsea Physic Garden and the Museum of Croydon. She runs a web resource for museum professionals focused on operations and Visitor Experience planning at www.therecoveryroomblog.com, for which she was shortlisted for a Museums and Heritage Award in 2021. Rachel writes for attractions website *Blooloop* on museum-focused projects, and has published an article on crisis management in *Museums International*, the International Council of Museums journal. She was named one of the world's top 50 museum influencers in 2020 by *Blooloop*. Today, Rachel is the Head of Hampton Court Palace for Historic Royal Palaces, where she oversees operational and experience delivery for visitors to Henry VIII's iconic pleasure palace.

About the Author

Acknowledgements

The list of people who have contributed their time and experience to the case studies in this book reads like a Who's Who of UK Visitor Experience, and I am exceptionally lucky – not to mention grateful – to know them, work with them and to share their work here.

Thank you so much to Kayleigh McMahon, Emma Hermon, Mel Oakley, Martin Devereaux, Carly Straughan, Jasmine Allen, Steven Jugg, James Rodliff, Susan Morrison, Oliver Burton, Ann Fiddler, Paul Griffiths, Liz Power, David Hingley and Clare Lane for being generous enough to share your thoughts and experiences with me. Thanks must also go to my editors Rhiannon Goddard and Maria Blyzinksy, as well as the many others who have inspired, advised and encouraged this book.

Introduction

Museums are for everyone. This is one of the most fundamental principles of working in museums today, and it's something that every single person working in the organisation plays a role in delivering.

When it comes to welcoming our audiences on site, and ensuring a great visit for everyone, our front-facing team members are at the coalface of delivering this principle. They are part of a team we have come to call 'Visitor Experience'.

Or, at least, some of us have come to call it that.

One of the hardest things about writing this book has been the definition of Visitor Experience. The team that looks after visitors, front-facing staff and the day-to-day operation of the museum has different names in different places. Visitor Services, Visitor Engagement, Operations, Front of House? Those are just the most common names; there are many more. Staff working on the frontline also have different names: Visitor Assistants, Warders, Hosts, Explainers, Front of House?

Not only that, but to add further confusion, the teams that make up this department might be different too. Sometimes these departments might include Security, or Retail, or Facilities Management. Sometimes they won't. Sometimes, in smaller museums, these are all the same people anyway.

We all have different preferences for what Visitor Experience means, but for the purposes of writing this book, I have had to come up with a couple of standard definitions.

For me, Visitor Experience is the name given to the people in the museum who look after the overall on-site visitor journey, ensuring that people who come to visit our museums have a safe, easy and enjoyable visit. I have come to split this responsibility into what I call the 'hard' Visitor Experience: the operational procedures, wayfinding, ticketing, and those twin banes of every Visitor Experience Manager's life, toilets and lifts. Then, we have the 'soft' Visitor Experience: our engagement with and delivery to our visitors; how we make our visitors feel welcome and personalise their experience through our interactions with them.

So, whilst sorting out definitions and names has been the tricky part of this book, the joyful, inspiring, life-affirming part has been writing about *how* we take on these responsibilities to look after the Visitor Experience.

We do this by knowing our visitors better than anybody else. We do it by understanding that people have different motives for coming to us, and respecting them all equally. We meet people where they are, whether they are looking for specialist information or just a lovely day out. We do it by knowing that museums really are for everyone.

Whilst many museums see their Visitor Experience teams as one department in a large organogram, for me Visitor Experience sits at the centre of the museum web, working with colleagues in other departments to make sure they can bring their ideas to life, whilst keeping the visitor at the centre of every decision made. In addition to this, the job can mean all sorts of other things. Sometimes it's doing quick and detailed sums around capacity and people movement, sometimes it just means bringing the right people together around the table, and more often than not it can mean asking 'have you thought about the toilets?' at regular and frequent intervals.

This book is aimed at Visitor Experience professionals across all these different facets of the job, or indeed anyone who is interested in the holistic visitor experience in museums. It's split into three parts, covering the creation, the day-to-day management and the future development of Visitor Experience. Every chapter included in this book is accompanied by a case study highlighting great practice across the sector. Each one has taught me that inspiration and creativity is abundant in our world, that great ideas can come from all sizes and types of museums, and most importantly, that the future of Visitor Experience is in safe hands.

PART 1

Creating the Visitor Experience

Although many of us work at museums and heritage sites that have been around a lot longer than we have, sometimes we will come across the opportunity to create a visitor experience from scratch. This might be in the form of a new exhibition or offer within an existing site, or when opening a brand-new attraction for the first time.

Creating a visitor experience from the beginning is an amazing opportunity. It allows you to set the tone of your offer and the culture of your workforce. It allows you to get all the processes and procedures in place exactly as you like them, without having to battle with pre-existing ways of doing things.

However, setting up everything from the beginning is also a lot of work. And, because many Visitor Experience professionals have been in this position as well, there's no need to reinvent the wheel in every area. This first part of the book allows you to learn from best practice when it comes to creating your visitor experience, using case studies from organisations such as the Postal Museum and the Ashmolean to help inform your work.

But this part isn't just for those starting from scratch. Going back to basics is a great way to audit a visitor experience you are already managing. So, whether you are an experienced Visitor Experience Manager or brand-new to the sector, there will be something you will find useful in this section.

Visitor Experience is all about people. Therefore, the first three chapters of this book explore the most important factor in delivering amazing visitor experiences: getting your Visitor Experience team in place. Using case studies from Margate Caves and Verdant Works: Scotland's Jute Museum, we'll explore how to recruit and induct staff and volunteers, using processes that build diverse and enthusiastic teams.

Then, we'll start to look at the experiences, beginning with a detailed look at visitor journey mapping. This tool can help us ensure we are considering our new experience (or our current ones) from the visitor point of view.

Finally, we'll take a look at setting up those nuts and bolts of the visitor experience: ticketing, capacities and queues, using a case study from the Stained-Glass Museum to show that great technological solutions don't have to break the bank.

CHAPTER 1

Recruiting Your Visitor Experience Team

> They had all the things I needed, because they could do customer service and they were passionate.
>
> (Kayleigh McMahon, Margate Caves)

Given that the most important element of delivering the visitor experience is the visitor-facing staff, it follows that the recruitment of that team will need to be considered with the utmost thought and care. In this chapter, we'll look at how you can attract great candidates, run a fair and inclusive recruitment process and consider different ideas for selecting your team.

Types of hiring

The first thing to think about is how you will be hiring your team; in other words, the contract they will be on.

There are many types of contracts that you might want to consider, depending on the seasonality of your operation. For example, if staff are only needed over the summer, it would make sense to have a fixed-term contract. However, if needs are more likely to flex throughout the year, it would be worth looking into a mix of permanent and casual contracts. For full-time employees who work shorter hours in the winter for operational reasons, think about annualised hours. This means that not only would they get paid the same all throughout the year, your costs stay even too.

Whatever type of contract is chosen, the important thing is that it works for the business and that it works for the employee. Zero-hour contracts are an example of where, historically, this has not happened. The abuse of zero-hour contracts is well documented. An interview published in *The Guardian* in 2017 reported that zero-hours workers can feel 'disposable' and even 'bullied' (Williams, 2017). It's true that if used properly these contracts can work for both parties; however, more often than not they can be seen as exploitative, especially if workers are expected to maintain availability without the promise of hours. Museums and visitor attractions have tended to move away from this kind of contract, and instead you should aim for an arrangement that benefits both the employer and the employee.

In the past few years, I've seen a lot of museums use agency staff for visitor-facing teams, and even been aware of organisations contracting out the whole department. Although larger museums may find this useful, due to the sheer numbers of staff they need, personally I would advocate against indirect hire for a number of reasons:

- Your visitor-facing team is the clearest expression of your brand and organisational values. You want them to represent the museum well, to feel engaged with the organisation and to pass on that positivity to visitors. I believe this starts with direct employment. If you wouldn't outsource your curators, interpretation team or marketing team, don't outsource your visitor experience teams.
- Outsourcing and agency use means less reliance on in-house management and more reliance on external forces when it comes to development and training. Why outsource such an important part of the visitor experience when you could have a direct impact on shaping it?
- It used to be that using agency staff was a lot cheaper than hiring staff directly. However, in the UK this has not been the case since 2010, when the Agency Workers Regulations came into law. Under this legislation, after 12 weeks agency workers are entitled to 'the same or no less favourable treatment for basic employment and working conditions' (UK Government, 2019). This includes pay. Therefore, there is no longer a large financial incentive to use agency staffing.
- Many organisations have been comforted by the notion that agency staff are employees of the agency rather than the museum. This idea should provide protection against any cases brought by the worker in regard to issues such as unfair dismissal. However, if agency staff are treated pretty much the same as directly hired staff (which, since 2010 they have to be in regard to pay and conditions) any legal protection offered by indirect employment is likely to be ineffective. I've seen numerous cases of agency workers successfully claiming employee status and bringing cases against the organisation, so I personally don't think legal protection has been a valid benefit of indirect hiring since 2010.

I know that there may be situations where indirect hiring is unavoidable: for example for large, short-term staffing needs, or if the museum is under a permanent recruitment freeze and positions need to be filled. However, where appointments are likely to last beyond 12 weeks, my opinion is that direct hire should always be the goal. Happily, many museums are now bringing former agency staff in-house, so hopefully large-scale indirect hiring is a thing of the past.

To summarise, show your Visitor Experience teams how important they are, and make them part of the museum family.

What to look for

If you're hiring Visitor Experience staff for the first time, there are a lot of good resources out there to help inform your planning. One helpful source in the UK is Fair Museum Jobs (FMJ), a grassroots movement whose objective is to establish a manifesto 'for museum job recruitment that is based on the principles of fairness, transparency, equity and inclusivity' (FMJ, 2021a).

Much of the guidance in the manifesto is applicable to the hire of Visitor Experience teams, and advice that I would support. For example, one of the areas it touches on is the need for academic qualifications in the museum sector:

> University Degrees, both undergraduate or postgraduate, must not be required as criteria on personal specifications. Where skills traditionally derived from academia are deemed a requirement for a role (such as subject specialism or aptitude at research, analysis, and source criticism and citation) these specific skills and knowledge areas should be required rather than blanket qualifications.
>
> (FMJ, 2021b)

This is an especially pertinent observation when it comes to Visitor Experience roles. A survey carried out in 2019 by advocacy group FOH Museums showed that the numbers of Visitor Experience staff with degrees has risen over recent years (FOH Museums, 2019). Whilst candidates with higher educational achievements obviously bring a wealth of knowledge into the organisation, it can also lead to lack of motivation in post, staff feeling unappreciated and under-used, and ultimately, high turnover. Additionally, whilst the sector is no doubt lucky to have well-educated and knowledgeable staff members in frontline teams, this does raise questions about the accessibility of such roles, and whether the sector is doing enough to provide entry-level routes into museums for a diverse range of candidates.

In 2016, the Museums Association (MA) commissioned a report called *Valuing Diversity: the case for inclusive museums*. Academic qualifications came up again in this research, with the report stating: 'Some people… feel that the sector holds on to a culture of over-professionalisation, with many practitioners overqualified for their role. This narrows entry to the workforce for people who don't take traditional academic routes' (MA, 2016, 14).

So, is a degree really needed for visitor-facing positions? I would argue that people skills and proactivity are characteristics that should be prioritised above academic qualifications. In fact, far from requiring Visitor Hosts at my organisation to have a history degree, we only actually ask for an interest in history. We can teach them the facts; it's far more important that we know candidates can demonstrate teamwork and people skills, whether those have been gained in the museum sector or not. Therefore, when writing the role description, focus on the skills and characteristics needed to do the job, and be sparing about what are considered to be 'essential' criteria. If a degree is absolutely critical for the role, always aim to include an 'equivalent experience' clause.

How to recruit fairly and inclusively

A big part of the above thinking is ensuring that we are making the route into museums as accessible as possible. Not only do we want to avoid any discrimination when it comes to recruitment, there are multiple benefits to diverse hiring. Museums can much better meet the needs of their audiences if they are as diverse as the population they serve, and with diverse recruitment comes different ideas, backgrounds and experience that can only enrich the work we do. Not only that, but it improves employee productivity and retention (Taylor, 2021).

Despite this, the UK museum workforce is currently not reflective of the broader population. The latest Arts Council England (ACE) report on disability in the workplace points out that although 18% of the working population in England are classed as disabled, only 4% of the workforce at National Portfolio Organisations and Major Partner Museums self-identify as disabled (ACE, 2017). Similarly, ACE's report *Equality, Diversity and the Creative Case* found that despite small increases, at 12%, non-white workers are still under-represented in museums, especially at leadership level (ACE, 2019).

So how can museums attract employees from a more diverse background? First, take some time to evaluate the diversity of your own organisation and think about what needs to be changed to more fully support employees from diverse backgrounds. There are some tools in the Museums Association report *Power and Privilege in the 21st Century Museum* that can help you carry out this evaluation (MA, 2017).

Practically speaking, there are programmes you can sign up to which will help you become more confident in diverse hiring. For example, UK employers can sign up to the government's Disability Confident scheme (UK

Government, 2016). This is a three-level course that helps employers attract and support disabled employees, and ultimately empower individuals to act as champions for disability-confident employment.

Making the requirements in job descriptions as accessible as possible has been discussed above. However, there may be other barriers to access that are unconsciously built into the application process. For example, FMJ advise: 'Vacancies should not close early due to volume of applications. If the closing date is extended, the extension and the reasons for it must be clearly communicated to existing applicants' (FMJ, 2021b).

When thinking about inclusive hiring, it's always good to look to other sectors to see if there is anything museums can learn. Tess C. Taylor at The Academy to Innovate HR (AIHR) has published *12 Inclusive Hiring Practices Your Organisation Should Implement*, and many of them are worth considering from a museum perspective. For example, Taylor advocates 'inclusive job descriptions' excluding gender-based language and terms (Taylor, 2021). From a museum point of view, FMJ support this, advising that recruiters make adverts 'clear and concise' and avoiding 'unnecessary jargon' (FMJ, 2021b). Taylor also advises expanding what you do with those adverts. If you advertise in the same kind of places year after year, you're likely to get the same kind of applicants. Broaden it out by working with job centres and back-to-work courses at local colleges.

As well as thinking carefully about what is needed from prospective employees, you should also think about what you can give to them. Consider how you are promoting your museum as an attractive place to work. If you are looking to increase diversity, make sure the application process walks the walk. This might be through a website that uses clear language, is digitally accessible and talks honestly about what you are doing to promote diversity and inclusion in your organisation. Whilst this can run the risk of coming off as tokenistic, Taylor advises a more genuine approach: 'Instead of stock photos that trivialise diversity, use authentic images of your team (with permission)' (Taylor, 2021).

One tip from the technology sector is to make recruitment panels more diverse. For example, tech giant Intel made it policy for recruitment panels to include managers from under-represented groups. 'Within two years, they managed to grow the number of hires with diverse backgrounds by 41%' (Taylor, 2021).

In order to remove any trace of discrimination from the recruitment process, many museums are investing in unconscious bias training for their workforce. As Museums Association (MA) research into inclusion in 2016 demonstrated, these biases can go even further than recruitment. 'This research demonstrates that unconscious bias not only impacts decisions related to recruitment and salary of individuals but also impacts investment in their ongoing development once inside an organisation' (MA, 2016, 13). Hopefully the roll out of such training schemes will mean that not only is the whole organisation more ready to increase the diversity of their staff, any unconscious barriers that may have stopped them doing will be reduced.

Examples of inclusive hiring schemes in museums

One way to increase routes into the sector is to explore paid internships. Manuel Charr, writing for *Museum Next*, uses the example of Create NY, a cross-institutional programme in New York cultural organisations that aimed to diversify their workforces. As part of this work, Brooklyn Museum launched a paid internship programme, which aimed to improve access and diversity by making opportunities open to everyone. 'After all, unpaid interns may gain a valuable foothold in the museum industry which can lead to great career paths but if only people who are financially secure can gain them, then this hardly breaks down traditional hierarchies' (Charr, 2019).

Another example is Museum Galleries Scotland (MGS), who have rolled out several schemes to increase diversity in museum and gallery workforces. One such scheme, Skills for Success, focused on delivering accredited work-based learning. MGS trained up sector professionals as assessors and verifiers to deliver vocational qualifications. Another scheme, the Heritage Horizons Traineeship programme, provided the opportunity for non-graduates from a range of backgrounds to attain vocational qualifications in Museums and Galleries Practice alongside workplace learning during a 12-month paid placement (MGS, 2021).

According to MGS:

> Since 2011, 78 learners have successfully completed placements in museums and galleries across Scotland. 87% have gone on to find employment, with roles including Museum Managers, Curators, Collections Assistants and Learning Managers. These vocational programmes have provided an alternative route of entry into the sector, improving training resources, and diversifying the workforce.
>
> (MGS, 2021)

The salary

Salary is another element of recruitment that can impact access, but there are so many issues attached to it that it deserves a whole section of this chapter on its own.

First, the primary rule is that salaries should always be listed. FMJ goes further and advises absolute clarity when it comes to part-time jobs – list both the annual salary and the pro-rata salary (FMJ, 2021b). If there is a mix of part-time, full-time roles and casual roles available, make this clear. UK salaries should conform to the Real Living Wage or London Living Wage, depending on location.

Low salaries are themselves a barrier to access, and this is widely acknowledged to be a problem in the museum world. In 2022, the Museums Association noted; 'Museum pay significantly lags behind the market and is on average 10% below comparator rates' (MA, 2022). To help keep consistency in the UK sector, the Association publishes salary guidelines, which are updated regularly.

The Guidelines set the salaries of Visitor Experience staff at approximately £18,500–20,800 p.a. (MA, 2022), whilst also making the point that these groups are more likely to be affected by sector low pay and other risks. 'This group is also among the most vulnerable to rising inflation costs and redundancy' (MA, 2022).

The selection process

The most important advice I can share for creating the candidate selection process is to make the process fit the role. Some organisations have extremely long application forms that need to be filled in through a complex online portal. Is this really necessary for the role you are looking for? I've found that it is possible to attract great candidates by making the application simpler, for example by asking for CVs only. It's crucial that if those CVs can be sifted without names and dates, to make sure that the selection is not affected by unconscious bias.

When it comes to the next stage, consider what you are asking people to do. If this is an entry-level position, don't put candidates through a follow-up interview. If they won't have to use PowerPoint in their role, don't make them use it in the interview. If they won't have to use Excel in their role, don't make them use it in the interview, and so on and so forth. In fact, I will go further and say that even the traditional interview, where one sits in front of a panel while the CV is picked over, is not the correct method to choose a Visitor Experience team member.

Go back to those critical skills and characteristics you identified in the role description. How can you best assess them in a selection process? When you're looking at engagement skills, presentation skills, and adaptability to dealing with a lot of different people, it soon becomes clear that a panel interview may not be the best method.

Today, many museums and visitor attractions are going down the route of holding assessment centres and recruitment days rather than traditional individual interviews. Not only does this significantly increase the number of applicants who can be invited, it allows you to see the candidates interact with each other in a group, along with other tasks you can throw in dependent on the job role, such as teamwork tasks and short talks or presentations. It's also a chance to tell them more about the role, give them a tour and even let them meet some of the current staff. In this way, an event like this becomes much more of a two-way process, and is a lot less intimidating and therefore more accessible than a traditional interview.

There may always have to be a short interview as part of this process; after all, we all need to ask those individual housekeeping questions about notice periods and holiday, as well as some competency-based questions if necessary. However, when it comes to interview questions, FMJ advise informing candidates in advance:

> Recruiting organisations must inform all candidates about the constitution of the interview panel and format of the interview ahead of time. Sharing interview questions is a commonly requested reasonable adjustment; and an increasing number of organisations are choosing to share interview questions with all candidates.
>
> (FMJ, 2021b)

Whether you choose to share questions in advance or not, my advice would be to make that interview process as short as possible for Visitor Experience roles. There are simply other selection activities that give a better idea of how a candidate will perform in a front-facing role. I've included some examples of these in Table 1.1 opposite. One caveat is that if candidates are required to prepare anything in advance, even if it's a minute-long presentation, make sure they are given plenty of time to do so.

After the selection

There are three stages of the post-selection journey you will have to consider as recruiting managers: the rejection, the references and the onboarding.

It's an unpleasant truth that as a manager you'll have to reject a lot more candidates than you hire. This process can often be awkward, but only you have the power to turn it from a disappointing experience into a rewarding, and ultimately positive, one through the use of feedback. I would encourage all recruiting managers to offer feedback to those they have interviewed. If possible, it's always great to be able to provide feedback on applications as

Table 1.1 *Selection process suggestions*

Working with others	Presentation skills	Visitor engagement
Work together to design a new theme park, garden, museum or exhibition.	Tell the group about the best visitor experience you've ever had and why it was so great.	
Egg drop – give your group an egg and assorted craft materials. They must work together to build a landing craft that will protect the egg from a drop within a certain timeframe.	Ask candidates to bring in one object that says something about them and deliver a three-minute presentation on it.	Ask candidates to share their best examples of service in a shop, café or visitor attraction.
The fox, the chicken and the bag of grain. The group works together to solve the problem of how to get all three items safely across the river in a small boat. Search online for the answer, or watch Episode 4, Season 1 of *The Office* (UK)!	Ask candidates to prepare a three-minute presentation about their favourite historical character.	Ask candidates to share their worst examples of service in a shop, café or visitor attraction.
Plane crash – the group have crash-landed and must rank the objects with them in order of importance. The order must be agreed on within a certain timeframe. There are many different versions of this game: just search 'group exercise plane crash' online for some examples.	Ask candidates to do a tour of the museum and then give a short presentation on the best thing they've seen.	Ask candidates to role-play a visitor scenario, such as a complaint.

well, although I understand that for large-scale recruitment drives that isn't always going to be feasible. The most important thing is not to make the offer of feedback if you're not actually going to follow up on it when asked.

As to when and how you do this, FMJ recommends 'not giving feedback at the same time as giving the recruitment outcome. Allow unsuccessful candidates time to absorb the result of the process before receiving feedback' (FMJ, 2021b). It's also important to think through what you are going to say, and this is where the notes you and your colleagues have made during the selection process really come into their own. Try and give some positive feedback as well as actionable things to work on, and be as honest as you can.

If you are providing feedback to unsuccessful internal candidates and offer up development opportunities as part of that process, make sure you follow through on that. There's nothing more demoralising than feeling unwanted at your current organisation. Alternatively, if you show interest in and care for your in-house talent even when they haven't been successful in recruitment, it will do a lot for morale and retention.

When it comes to references, make sure you are asking for what you need, and not gathering personal data for the sake of it. In particular, advice is now tending away from asking about previous sickness or parental leave. FMJ say 'we advise that you must not ask for sickness absence reports as this is ableist – discriminating against disabled candidates, or those with any long-term health condition' (FMJ, 2021b). It also doesn't necessarily give you a good indication of how the candidate in question is going to perform with you: you're not getting the context of what was going on in their lives when in that previous role. I've also heard more and more anecdotal evidence of managers refusing to answer these questions when giving references, and I suspect that within a few years it will cease to be a common question. Another unnecessary question is asking someone what salary they received in their previous job. Again, this is no indication of how they will perform in their new role, and is therefore being phased out.

Finally, when someone is offered the job, don't leave them hanging. Make sure the onboarding is a welcoming process and keep the lines of communication open. Make sure they have all the information they need about their first day, where to go and what initial training they will receive. In short, make them feel like part of the organisation right from the start.

Case Study 1: Recruiting a new team for Margate Caves

In 2019, Margate Caves in Kent reopened to the public after a 15-year closure. This necessitated a whole new recruitment drive, and a new way of thinking about hiring Visitor Experience staff for General Manager Kayleigh McMahon.

When thinking about what candidates she needed, McMahon thought hard about the visitor offer and how the local community could both support the Caves, and be supported in turn by the organisation:

'I knew that I wanted to be supporting local people and I wanted locals working here' says McMahon. However, despite a fairly active museum and heritage landscape in Kent, teams at other local attractions were well-established 'so there wasn't necessarily a lot of movement heritage-wise in Margate' (McMahon, 2021). This, combined with widespread long-term unemployment in the area, meant that McMahon would have to cast her net as widely as possible to get what she needed.

'So, having seen something similar done at a previous role, I just put out a really basic customer service role description, and asking for just a vague interest in history,' McMahon explains. 'I didn't put any work experience requirement, it was more focused on knowing what good customer service looked like'.

After asking for a CV and expression of interest, McMahon invited every single person who applied to a recruitment day, designed to be 'a little less formal, a little less intimidating' than a traditional interview. 'Margate has endemic unemployment, so I didn't want it to be a big scary process', she explains. 'They were asked when they came to the recruitment day to come prepared to talk about somewhere they'd visited that they really enjoyed and why someone else should visit there. And they had a tour of the caves; they all sat and chatted, then they did their presentations, and then we took them off one at a time and did a little five-minute stand-up interview'.

The interview section of the recruitment day was short, including questions such as 'What does good customer service look like to you?' as well as the usual practical questions covering booked holiday and notice periods. However, the majority of the process was focused on ensuring the candidates were able to get a good idea of what Margate Caves were all about, and to demonstrate their interpersonal and presentation skills.

Even the informal parts of the day were useful. 'Two of my colleagues stayed with the group while we took the person off to do the informal interview, and actually it was really helpful to see how people interacted with each other,' McMahon says. 'Some people knew each other, some people didn't, so seeing how people dealt with a stranger in front of them, when you're doing a role like we do, in front of house, is actually very helpful'.

The outcome was a valued and diverse staff pool. 'I ended up with an artist, someone who was currently working in a pharmacy and previously had only ever worked in the retail side of things, and someone who had been unemployed for a while because of children, and previous to that, had been a cleaner, and had worked in a butchers', McMahon says. In previous organisations, she explains, these candidates might not have even got to interview. 'But actually, they had all the right things I needed, because they could do customer service and they were passionate about the caves, and about Margate and Thanet and actually it brought a different kind of angle.'

When the new intake started, the value of this became even clearer. 'We trained them in things, but they also taught us stuff,' McMahon says. 'I'm from Kent, but I'm not from Margate. I learned things from them about the local history, and the local lay of the land.' It also brought benefits in the shape of longer-term relationship building. Some candidates weren't quite ready for the position, but joined as volunteers, and were able to build up their confidence. In fact, as McMahon explains, 'one of my volunteers that I got from that day ended up working for me this year on a summer contract.'

By opening up the recruitment process and widening the pool as much as possible, Margate Caves has been able to bring diverse backgrounds, experience and knowledge into its Visitor Experience team, and at the same time, support their local community with skills development, relationship building and employment opportunities: the definition of a win-win.

CHAPTER 2

Delivering a Great Induction

> How we welcome new colleagues to the Visitor Experience team is just as important as how we welcome our visitors.
>
> (Emma Hermon, The Ashmolean Museum)

Once you have recruited your dream Visitor Experience team, the next step is planning for their induction training. Delivering a thorough and well thought-through induction is crucial; both to welcoming new colleagues to your organisation and to giving them the tools they need to get started in their new job. However, it's important to know that we shouldn't let the learning stop there: training and professional development should be an ongoing part of any job. We'll discuss that more in Part 3.

The induction period is of the utmost importance when it comes to setting the right tone for the employee experience. For museums that are open all year round, the period right before new staff start work is the longest uninterrupted period of time you will get to work with your team away from the floor, so it's well worth making the most of it. Most critically, in the induction period, you demonstrate the culture in which you expect your team to work, so the negative impact of delivering a rushed, ill-considered induction period can be huge.

Some museum and heritage organisations I have worked with or for spend up to a couple of weeks on new staff induction, and some as little as a couple of hours! Of course, every situation is different, and you will need to consider the amount of information you need to impart to your new team. One new staff member will obviously take less time, but if I am inducting a new cohort of Visitor Experience staff, I will probably set aside a week. In group inductions you are not only imparting the tools and information new staff need, you are facilitating the formation of important relationships: professional connections between you and your team, between them and their new colleagues, but also personal friendships and relationships that may outlast their time at the museum. It's probably the most valuable week they will spend at the organisation.

Each organisation has different needs and will organise different inductions. However, here are some general prompts that might help you prepare and plan for engaging, memorable and valuable induction periods.

What do you need your new team to know?

If you are starting from scratch, a good first step would be to make a list of all the things you think your team will need to know. There are lots of practical things that have to be covered as part of an operational induction. Below is a list of the things that would be a good start, but certainly won't be exhaustive:

- familiarisation with the spaces they will be working in
- till systems training
- fire evacuation and other emergency training
- safeguarding
- radio training
- data protection
- health and safety training (including manual handling)
- social media policy
- who they will be working with (the hierarchy of the organisation)
- operational policies such as lost children and vulnerable adults, unattended items, first aid.

But it's not just about the practicalities. There are also cultural elements to consider, such as the values and goals of the organisation and how the Visitor Experience teams fit into that. Frontline staff exemplify the personality of your museum; so how they talk to visitors, how they engage with them and even how they upsell to them all matters. If you can tie all these things together in the induction period, they can start to see how valuable they are to the organisation. So, when you are introducing the soft skills of Visitor Experience, such as upselling and engagement, make sure it all flows from the core of what the museum is trying to do.

Some of the induction content might be specific to your organisation. At Historic Royal Palaces, new Hosts don't have to bring a knowledge of history with them to their role. We work with the curators to give them all the information they need by delivering wonderful tours and talks for them during their induction period. However, we also find that the team build on that knowledge as they go through the time, often becoming more knowledgeable than long-standing staff! So, if your museum is focused on a very specific subject don't get too hung up on trying to stuff them full of all available knowledge during a short induction period. Instead, give them the basics and inspire a passion in them to keep learning as they go; that way, it is far more likely to sink in.

Finally, think about when you first started to work at the organisation. What things seemed scary or daunting? What do you wish someone had told you? Breaking down acronyms, making sure new staff can find their way around the buildings and getting them introduced to all the new faces they are going to be working alongside – these are all really important parts of the induction.

Think carefully about the order and delivery

If you are doing a lengthy group induction, you have to expect that attention will wander at certain points. There are several reasons why this can happen, even if your museum is the most interesting place in the world! First of all, starting a new job is hard. It takes a lot of mental energy to learn so much new information in a short space of time, so tiredness and lethargy can be an issue. Secondly, if the induction is a big group, it can be easy to hide and sit back without interacting too much. Thirdly, with the best will in the world, not every topic that needs to be covered (particularly some of the statutory modules) will be heart-stopping, edge-of-the-seat material.

However, you can alleviate a lot of these issues by thinking about the order and delivery of your sessions. For example, try to mix up modules so that there isn't too much dry, 'sitting and listening' material on the same day. If you are spending the morning doing classroom style induction, make sure you get the group on their feet in the afternoon. This will also help you avoid the after-lunch slump.

Make sure the group hears an assortment of voices during their induction training. Not only does this introduce variety into the schedule, it means that they get to meet as many of their new colleagues as possible. This is invaluable in breaking down those back-of-house/front-of-house barriers before they get a chance to build up. Of course, this means more co-ordination, but the effort is worth it. At Kew Palace, we used to schedule our speakers for the March induction in December to make sure the right people were training on the right topics.

Some of the modules might be pick-and-mix style, in that they can be dropped into different days depending on schedules. Others are more important to place carefully. For example, I mentioned above that you want to set the culture by engaging new staff in the goals and values of their new organisation. It's good to do this early in the programme so that all the other content flows from that. Similarly, you might want to do ice-breaking or team-building exercises early on to get the new team familiar with each other. Finally, remember to schedule in plenty of breaks and down time, when the new team can get to know each other on their own terms.

Consider different learning styles and mix it up!

In a team of new recruits, learning styles may vary considerably. This might be something that you can actually adapt the induction to assist with. For example, a new recruit might let you know that they have some learning needs that could be supported with changes such as receiving written materials in advance or printing handouts on different coloured paper. But even if you aren't approached with a particular need, it's important to bear in mind that not everyone learns the same way. Try to incorporate a variety of teaching styles within the induction week: not every module needs to be delivered via PowerPoint. Here are some suggestions for how different types of material can be delivered:

- classroom-style sessions
- interactive hands-on sessions (great for practical topics like manual handling)
- role playing (great for simulating visitor behaviour in situations such as evacuation)
- tours (great for learning about the museum and its history)
- group work (great for team building and co-production)
- quizzes and games
- e-learning
- short films
- self-led learning (great for building up knowledge at their own pace).

Whichever you choose, the point is to ensure a mix of activity, so that everyone has a chance to let the content sink in and to ask any questions.

Include some on-the-job activity

One of the best ways of learning is on the job. When I was at the Natural History Museum, we would always follow up our induction week with a couple of days of shadowing: buddying up a new Visitor Assistant with a more experienced team member to really learn the ropes. This is important because it's where the new team member gets to grips with the ins and outs of the day, and gets to practise the skills they have learnt in a real situation – but with some stabiliser wheels attached.

There are other benefits to this approach too. Andy Nyberg, Director of Visitor Services at the Art Institute of Chicago, has spoken about how he feels this is the best way to teach new staff the soft skills they need to engage with visitors:

> We've found that teaming up with someone who's good at dealing with customers is the most effective way to train . . . We tried motivational speakers and corporate customer-service training, but most of our employees are graduate students and they felt they were being talked down to.
>
> (Lila Wallace – Reader's Digest Fund, 2000, 35)

When I was at Kew Palace, which had a smaller, seasonal team, we found this approach hard to do because all the team start at the same time. So, my management team and I had to clear our diaries for the first couple of weeks of the season and take on the role of buddies ourselves, being present on the floor as a support and positioning ourselves in key areas where we know it can be daunting the first time out.

Project the values you want your team to reflect

This comes back to that all-important task of setting the culture for your team early on. In fact, this starts in the recruitment process, as we discussed in Chapter 1. But the induction period is where you really start to bed that in. Remember, the new staff member has chosen to work for your museum, maybe because of how the organisation was sold to them during the recruitment process. During the induction week, the new recruits will decide whether or not that was false advertising; and they'll decide based on the behaviour of the staff delivering their induction modules, and the quality of the welcome they get.

Delivering a great induction takes a lot of organisation and preparation beforehand, but it also requires 100% of your attention whilst it's happening. It's not just about switching it on when you're delivering the training yourself; you also need to be fully present when you are greeting the team each morning, shepherding them from place to place, answering questions and introducing them to new people. It takes a lot of energy, but it's so worth doing properly. Getting to know the new team and being fully there for them in those first few days builds up the two-way trust and respect that is needed to have a great working relationship for however long they will be with you;

and it models the behaviour you want them to pass on to museum stakeholders as well.

Take the example of the Disney team training, which is built on this very idea:

> The Disney core belief is that a happy team (or cast) member makes a happy guest, which delivers the whole vision. If your volunteers out front are enthusiastic and passionate, they will communicate that to the visitor. If they are feeling hard done by, neglected, unwanted and pressurised, guess what? They'll communicate that too.
>
> (Wallace, 2013)

Inspire as well as instruct (but be realistic)

I think it's really important to build moments of awe into your induction alongside all the practical things you need to deliver. Museums and heritage sites are unique places to work; they aren't shops or cafés or offices. They hold inspiring collections and contain unbelievable histories. Use that to your advantage during induction and build excitement in your team about the fascinating stories they are going to be able to share with visitors and the amazing spaces they get to work in.

When I used to take our new recruits at the Natural History Museum on their first tour of the galleries, I'd always make sure to build in a bit of a sense of wonder. I'd take them up to the Giant Sequoia specimen, which is situated on a bridge high above the central hall. After I'd spoken about the tree, I'd get the new team to turn around, where they were met with an amazing view of the central hall architecture, the Diplodocus specimen and the beautiful painted ceiling. I'd invite them to just take a moment to drink in the beautiful building they were about to work in. It was a view that never failed to awe.

Saying all of that, be careful to remain realistic about what the job is. It's natural to want to raise excitement, but don't tell your team they are going to be spending all their time having deep conversations with visitors if, in reality, there are going to be a lot more busy days where their jobs become very operationally focused instead. Don't tell them they will get time to research their own projects if that's not true. Things like queue management and wayfinding are a really important part of the job, and that's fine as long as people are prepared for that. Be realistic about the role and make it clear what the expectations are.

Evaluate and review

Like anything, inductions can become stale if they are not evaluated and reviewed to ensure they are fit for purpose. The first stage of this evaluation should happen within the induction period itself, and this is primarily to ensure that the training you are delivering has worked and that your team are ready to head out onto the floor.

You can carry out this check by making it a fun and high-energy part of the induction; like a group quiz. Not only is this a bonding experience for the team, and a nice session to end induction week on, it lets you make sure that the basic facts have sunk in and ensure that your new team have been engaged with the content of your induction.

You will also need to think about longer-term evaluation. We did an annual induction at Kew Palace, and after every season my management team and I sat down and reviewed how we think the induction and subsequent season went before trying to plan the new one. As a result, I don't think we ever delivered two inductions that have ever been the same. We were constantly developing content; adding new sessions and making changes that could better support our Host team.

A big part of this development is capturing timely feedback from the participants. You will of course get a sense of how the induction is going just from the energy in the room, but some surveys and feedback forms where people can give anonymous feedback is really useful for evaluating which of the modules went well and which could use a little work.

You can also ask these questions further down the line. With a few months of work under their belt, your team might be able to let you know how prepared they were by their induction, and on reflection, what more they needed to know. They might also be more comfortable giving you this feedback once they have got to know you, as opposed to being fresh in to their new jobs!

However you get feedback, make sure that when you start preparing for a new induction, you are pausing to reflect on previous experience and learning any lessons you can. The induction you deliver next will be totally unique: for that team, in that moment and fitted for their needs. It's that sort of care that will start them out on the right path, and allow them to create the visitor experiences your museum wants to deliver.

Case Study 2: Induction at the Ashmolean Museum

At the Ashmolean Museum in Oxford, Head of Visitor Experience Emma Hermon puts great stress on delivering a fantastic induction. 'How we welcome new colleagues to the Visitor Experience team is just as important as how we welcome our visitors' she says.

'From the moment they come through the door, we want them to feel part of the team, that their contributions matter and they can make a difference' (Hermon, 2022).

Hermon knows a new environment can be overwhelming, and makes it the first priority to familiarise new staff with the spaces they will be working in. 'Knowing where the welfare facilities and lifts are and the quickest route to the café, are frequent questions so giving the team confidence and time to work out how to get around is our initial focus.' Therefore, a knowledge of what is important to the visitor is also key to creating an effective induction.

New elements have been built in over time through evaluation and review. For example, Hermon explains that in the current training, 'an important part is the PROTECT duty which has led to us also focusing on security training and effective collaboration with the security team.'

After spending a few days getting their heads around the operational aspects of the role, staff are given the chance to put the theory into practice by shadowing more experienced colleagues. Hermon explains: 'This practical approach gives them a real insight to the role and helps reinforce expectations and enables them to ask questions and meet the visitors with support of experienced colleagues.'

CHAPTER 3

Volunteering and the Visitor Experience

> It's not just a piece of paper telling visitors the history; it's somebody who lived and breathed it.
>
> (Mel Oakley, Dundee Heritage Trust)

Many museums across the world would not be able to offer the experience they do if it wasn't for the support of their volunteers. This support can range from a volunteer offer that adds value to the operation of a full staff team, to an entirely volunteer-run and -managed organisation. Wherever your museum sits on that spectrum, there's no doubt that volunteering is such a huge part of any museum visitor experience that it deserves its own chapter.

In the following pages, we'll explore the use of volunteers in delivering the visitor experience, and how you can get the best out of your volunteer team. For the purposes of this, I'll be focusing on how to manage a volunteer team alongside paid staff, although I know there are many small museums that are run entirely on a voluntary basis. Hopefully, some of the advice below will be useful for all concerned.

How to use volunteers

One of the first questions when considering volunteering in museums is how or when to use volunteers.

There are many reasons to bring volunteers into your organisation. They may bring new skills, knowledge and experience that you don't currently have in your employee pool. They widen your reach as an organisation, because if volunteers are socialising, gaining skills or having new experiences through you, it's all part of your engagement. This can then spread further, as the National Council of Volunteering Organisations (NCVO) point out on their website: 'Volunteers are often part of the communities you work or fundraise in. By giving them a great experience, you can inspire them to become your greatest advocates' (NCVO, 2021f).

One reason that shouldn't be a factor in using volunteers is the idea of 'free labour'. This motivation can arise (unsaid or not) in museums in times of financial stress, for example after the lockdowns caused by the COVID-19 pandemic. As the Heritage Volunteering Group (HVG) have stated:

> [After COVID-19] there are concerns about job substitution, replacement and displacement and the role volunteers will be asked to play in the face of job cuts. We do not support the replacement of paid roles with volunteers; however, we do believe that organisations should consider volunteers as part of their wider workforce.
>
> (HVG, 2021, 10)

This point is also picked up by grassroots campaign group Fair Museum Jobs (FMJ), who, as part of their manifesto, state: 'Voluntary positions must not be used to replace roles which were previously paid, or which carry duties and responsibilities one would normally expect from a paid role' (FMJ, 2021b).

Not only is the use of volunteers in lieu of paid staff ethically and legally questionable, it is, as anyone who has ever managed volunteers will know, an absolutely false economy. The Association of Independent Museums (AIM) puts it best, when it describes volunteer time as a 'gift': 'Unlike many gifts, though, this gift comes with responsibilities for the recipient, since running a successful volunteer programme takes both time and resources for the organisation' (AIM, 2021).

Managing volunteers generally takes more time, energy and experience than managing paid staff. This might be because you are dealing with a more diverse set of needs, motivations and prior experience, because volunteers have more social expectations from their role, or because they might need more supervision or assistance. However, I don't mean any of that to be understood as a negative. As long as you think of volunteering as part of the engagement work of your museum, rather than unpaid workers, you will find that they add enormous value to your team and to your visitors.

Below are just some of the ways in which volunteers are being used right now across the museum and heritage sector to add value to the visitor experience:

- positioned in historic houses or museum galleries to engage visitors with the content of the exhibitions and increase their knowledge and interest
- conducting guided tours
- leading object handling or other activities
- helping to sell tickets, or in the café or gift shop

- helping with on-site preservation or conservation projects, talking to visitors about the vital work of the museum
- driving or demonstrating heritage vehicles or machinery
- in costumed roles, engaging visitors with living history
- helping visitors orientate themselves around a historic site or museum
- talking about their lived experience around a particular topic or location
- retired members of staff who use volunteering as a way to keep their love of a topic alive and keep sharing their knowledge.

We'll explore a great example of the last point in the case study at the end of the chapter.

A volunteer strategy

If you make the decision to take on and manage volunteers, it's important to take some time to think about your approach to volunteering as an organisation. Doing this will ensure that you are keeping your organisational goals in mind as you embark on your volunteering programme. For example, is one of your organisational goals to target a younger audience? How can your volunteering programme support this goal?

Taking the time to think your approach through will also mean that you can problem-solve before problems occur, ensure that you have considered what the volunteer journey is going to look like for your organisation and, importantly, have the resource to support this. As HVG have said, '[Volunteers'] ingenuity and support will be central to creating new and innovative solutions that not only allow our sector to survive but to thrive. To do this, though, heritage organisations must possess the skills and culture that allows us to fully leverage volunteer talent' (HVG, 2021, 2).

Despite this critical need, a study carried out in 2021 by HVG and Historic England found that senior roles that look after volunteering as a specialism are rare in the sector and that 40% of UK museum and heritage organisations have no volunteering strategy (HVG, 2021, 6).

If your organisation is one of that 40%, consider that developing a strategy is a great way of thinking through the resources and processes you'll need to a support a volunteering programme. You can find online resources to help you create one on the Association of Independent Museums (AIM) website (https://aim-museums.co.uk) or the Group for Education in Museums (GEM) website (https://gem.org.uk). However, it doesn't need to be as formal as creating a written strategy. The important thing is that you take the time to think through your approach before recruiting volunteers, and ask yourself certain questions, such as:

- How will volunteering support the goals of the organisation?
- What are the long-term aims for our volunteering programme?
- What barriers are in place that might prevent us accomplishing this?
- How will we know when this has been accomplished?
- What are the tasks and roles that we want volunteers to take on?
- How will we recruit volunteers?
- What skills do we need from volunteers?
- What training will we give volunteers?
- Are we welcoming and inclusive to volunteers with diverse needs and experiences?
- Does our safeguarding policy cover young people and vulnerable adults when they are volunteering with us?
- Who will look after the volunteers and is any additional training needed to support this?
- How will we co-ordinate the volunteer admin, such as rotas and expenses? Do we need software?
- How will we recognise and reward volunteers?
- How will we measure volunteer performance?
- How will we resolve any performance issues?
- How will we gather feedback and suggestions from our volunteers?

Whether your strategy is formal or informal, the NCVO advises that it is reviewed at least every year to ensure that your volunteer programme is still going in the direction you want it to. 'Reviewing your strategy will help you respond to trends and changes in volunteering. It'll help you overcome challenges and develop volunteering further in your organisation' (NCVO, 2021e).

Volunteer recruitment

Once you have figured out your strategy for volunteering, your next step is to think about recruitment. For this, you will first have to decide what the volunteer role is going to be. This will need to be clear for both the organisation and the volunteers; in fact, museum accreditation requires you to have agreements with your volunteers (AIM, 2021) and is also advised by FMJ: 'Appropriate volunteer agreements should be in place between volunteers and hosting organisations, so that the expectations of both parties are understood' (FMJ, 2021b). In these agreements, volunteer roles should be distinct from the paid staff role: 'Be careful to create a clear distinction between employee and volunteer roles, as failure to do so could mean that a volunteer could claim worker or employee status and be eligible to receive the National Minimum Wage in return for their work' (AIM, 2021).

I've always found it useful to follow a couple of simple rules to ensure these distinctions are met. For example, in a museum that is staffed by both paid employees and volunteers, only paid staff should play a role in emergency evacuation and management. In general, volunteers should be added value, rather than have an operationally critical role within the museum.

The role should be stated in a way that is as accessible and inclusive as possible. Much of the advice for writing accessible job adverts in Chapter 1 will apply here, for example not including requirements for skills that aren't critical to the role. AIM also advises writing the role description or advert in 'simple language to ensure documents accessible for those whose first language isn't English or those with disabilities or cognitive processing conditions' (AIM, 2021).

One critical difference between volunteer adverts and paid staff adverts is that you might want to ensure that volunteers don't end up out of pocket, by paying them travel and other expenses. If this is the case, make sure this is clear in the initial advert (AIM, 2021; FMJ, 2021b). Also think carefully about how much time you are asking for. Asking for a large time commitment might drastically cut down the amount of people the volunteer role appeals to.

If you are looking to attract younger volunteers, as many museums are keen to, consider what skills development younger people can gain from the role, and promote those aspects when you advertise. For example, at Ripon Museum in Yorkshire a young volunteers' club was set up to provide support with policy making and change, as well as practical operational support on the ground. However, the opportunities for skills development are the real draw for joining the club, which 'combines developing heritage specific skills, like interpretation of historical resources and object handling, with transferrable skills such as working in teams, interacting with visitors and event organisation' (Hunwick-Brown, 2021).

Both AIM (https://aim-museums.co.uk) and the NCVO (www.ncvo.org.uk) give lots of good advice and example resources for recruiting and attracting volunteers, so I'd advise going through both websites if this is something you are doing for the first time.

When the time comes to select volunteers, don't get too carried away and make the interview too formal, or take up too much of their time. As the NCVO say, 'people are offering a gift of time, not seeking paid employment' (NCVO, 2021d). Also remember that potential volunteers are coming to check your museum out, just as much as you're going to check them out. The best thing you can do at a volunteer selection event is give them a great taste of what volunteer life at your museum is going to be. So, you might want to take potential volunteers on tour or show them behind the scenes.

It might also be a good idea to let them informally meet some current volunteers and staff at the recruitment event. This way they can ask any questions informally and get a feel for the organisational culture. Also, build in a bit of time for potential volunteers to speak to each other. You might even find that this social element takes up the majority of the event, but that's okay: many people choose to volunteer for social reasons, so it's good that this element is prioritised. In addition, by observing potential volunteers interacting with each other, you'll get a good idea of how they might engage with visitors when they're out on the floor.

You might not want to select every volunteer at the event, and that's okay too. The NCVO advise:

> It's important to tell the applicant the reasons that you're not accepting them as a volunteer. You can also suggest that the nearest Volunteer Centre may have more suitable roles for them. Applicants may also decide they don't want to volunteer for your organisation after all. In this case, ask the applicant for their reasons. This insight may prove helpful for future recruitment.
>
> (NCVO, 2021d)

Managing and developing volunteers

There are several aspects of managing volunteers that come under legal frameworks you might already have in place. In any case, it's good to review these aspects before bringing volunteers on board, including insurance, policies such as health and safety, data protection and safeguarding and of course risk assessments and any emergency procedures in place, including evacuation plans and crisis management plans. As mentioned above, I don't think it's appropriate that volunteers have a formal role in evacuation and emergency management, but they should still be included in plans. For example, how would you account for all your volunteers on site if something happened? Where should they go as a place of safety?

By far the most time-consuming (but also rewarding) aspect of volunteer management is the direct supervision. As AIM state, 'one of the key factors that drives volunteer engagement is the quality of the training and supervision provided' (AIM, 2021). NCVO suggest making expectations about supervision clear by using volunteer agreements to set out what organisations will offer volunteers (NCVO, 2021d). However, it's important that this isn't a contract; it's less formal than that. Talk about hopes and expectations rather than musts (NCVO, 2021d).

Even if you don't use volunteer agreements, it's important to clearly set out what the volunteer programme will look like: what you expect from volunteers, what they can expect from you, what training and support they will receive, what benefits they can look forward to (free entry or expenses?) and the content of the policies they need to be aware of. An induction checklist might help keep track of everything that needs to be shared with your new volunteer group.

Throughout your volunteers' time with you, clear communications processes and channels will need to be maintained. If you don't have regular feedback sessions built into the calendar you can find that issues can build up and grow out of proportion, or that volunteers feel they have to access their management team in a way that might not always be appropriate, such as out of hours. Make sure volunteers know that there are times and places to feed back any issues or suggestions, and do this in an authentic way: this information will be critical to developing your volunteer programme, and the visitor experience, further.

For example, before every season at Kew Palace, we used to send out a survey to all existing volunteers, asking them how they felt the previous season went and what changes they would like to see. Then, we held a coffee morning before the season started, where we could let them know what the new season was going to hold, how we had incorporated their feedback and talk through any questions or concerns. This meant that rather than assuming the operation would continue in the same way it had done before, volunteers approached the new season with a fresh frame of mind and clear expectations of the year ahead. This format worked for our seasonal offer at Kew, but there might be other communications processes and channels you want to consider for your organisation, such as:

- monthly volunteer meetings
- suggestion boxes
- one-to-ones
- online message boards.

How you manage this will depend on the size and shape of your team. The most important thing to bear in mind is to set expectations about communication right from the start.

Another key part of volunteer management is training. There is often concern that volunteers shouldn't receive training that is too similar to that of employees; however, NCVO dispute this:

> Depending on your resources, volunteers may get the same training as a paid member of staff. Keep training relevant and appropriate to the volunteer's role. This avoids taking up too much of the volunteer's time. It also makes sure training isn't seen as a perk or reward, which could make the volunteering look like paid work.
>
> (NCVO, 2021c)

When planning training, think carefully about the mix of skills and experience you might be dealing with. Volunteers, like paid staff, will have a variety of learning styles which needs to be taken into consideration. They might not necessarily have the skills you would require of paid employees, for example proficiency in using e-learning platforms. Ensuring any courses are fit for all and work with their availability rather than putting increased pressure on them will help volunteers engage with training and get the most out of it.

It's also important to remember that volunteers, like paid staff, can learn informally via their paid colleagues or through other volunteers. You will want to encourage this, as sharing and developing new skills is an important part of why many people volunteer. Encourage volunteers to work together rather than separately and try to involve them in planning conversations and ideas sharing as much as possible.

Retention, recognition and development

Once you have a volunteer team in place, keep checking in with your volunteers to make sure they are happy with how things are going. NCVO advise that 'the best way to keep volunteers is to make sure what they do meets their motivation for giving their time. Each volunteer will have different reasons for volunteering. Be flexible and open to meeting your volunteers' needs where possible' (NCVO, 2021a).

It might be possible to meet volunteers' needs over time with further development. If a volunteer shows particular skill in a specific area, or brings with them relevant experience from the outside world, try offering them more responsibility. For example, they could help train new volunteers, co-ordinate social events or lead on developing a new visitor offer.

Over time, you might have to deal with some difficult issues that arise within your volunteer team. On their website, NCVO offer some options in dealing with volunteer performance issues. These include: reviewing and revisiting the volunteer agreement, additional training or support, including a 'buddy' system, changing tasks or offering a new role (NCVO, 2021b). However, there may be times when the volunteer relationship is just not working and both parties have to go their separate ways. If this does happen, take whatever steps you can to frame the parting in a positive way. Act on any lessons learned and give them feedback that might be useful in the future. Remember, just because they aren't actively volunteering with you doesn't mean they won't be a future visitor or advocate for your museum.

Finally, even when things are running smoothly, it's important to consistently recognise the contribution your volunteers are making. This is different from a quid pro quo situation: although technically you should not be rewarding volunteers for unpaid work, you can and should take the time to recognise what they do. Recognition can be as simple as verbally thanking them at the end of each shift, including them in wider recognition from senior management or passing on good visitor feedback. However, it's good to think about the motivation for volunteering and how recognition can play into that. If your volunteers love a social occasion, how about organising an annual party? If they can't get enough of history, can you arrange a reciprocal tour for another organisation? If you're not sure, try asking the volunteers themselves how they would like their good work to be recognised – you might get some surprising answers!

So, whatever the size and shape of your volunteer team, taking the time to think through your approach to volunteering by considering the themes above will really help you prepare, organise and ultimately create the best experience for everyone who engages with your museum.

Case Study 3: Lived experience at Verdant Works: Scotland's Jute Museum

Volunteers are used in a number of roles at Dundee Heritage Trust (DHT), the conservation charity that looks after the RSS Discovery and Verdant Works: Scotland's Jute Museum. Some of them take on archive and conservation tasks, whilst others directly contribute to the visitor experience by acting as guides or costumed hosts. What exactly they talk about depends on the needs of the visitor, as Curator Mel Oakley explains: 'They make sure people don't miss things, and maybe give them a bit more background information and explain it in a way that works for them. It means that they can give a really tailored experience to the visitor' (Oakley, 2021).

However, at Verdant Works, the specifics of Dundee's heritage can be demonstrated and explained in an extra-special way. At the height of the 19th century, Dundee was home to over 150 jute companies, with mills like Verdant Works employing approximately 500 people. Many of the employees were women, leading to Dundee being dubbed 'she-town', where women went out to earn a living whilst the men (or 'kettle-bilers') stayed at home and raised the children. The jute industry dominated Dundee until the mid-20th century, when India became the primary manufacturing centre. However, despite its later decline, jute has shaped the urban landscape of Dundee and remains an important defining characteristic of the city today (DHT, 2022).

Verdant Works opened as a museum to the public in 1996 (DHT, 2022) and since then has been engaging visitors with life and conditions in the jute mills. Examples of mill machinery are still on display, and are often brought to life by volunteer machine demonstrators. One of those demonstrators is Lily, now in her 80s, who is the last remaining volunteer to have worked in the Dundee mills when they were operational. 'Lily's the last working weaver,' Oakley explains. '[She] can tell [visitors] that the mills were dirty places to be; that it was hard work; that they were poor, but there was a sense of community . . . It's not just a piece of paper telling them that; it's somebody who lived and breathed it.'

Oakley says that this difference is even more acute when it comes to working the machines. 'It's quite interesting, the dynamic between Lily and the other machine operators, because the machine operators give a demonstration of how the machines work, Lily works the machine. It's very subtle, but there is that difference. It's not a demonstration. She just shows them what she would have done when she was working in the mills.' Lily's professionalism and workmanship are such that Oakley can tell the difference between cloth produced by Lily and the other machine demonstrators just by looking.

People like Lily are all the more valuable because the experience they are giving visitors is, sadly, a finite one. The knowledge and understanding of the industrial revolution as lived experience is on the decline. 'I think all industrial museums are having this experience now, where we're losing this understanding' says Oakley. At Verdant Works, this means a future where 'the visitor experience is going to be demonstrations as opposed to [someone] working the machine as they would have worked it in their working life . . . In the next 10–15 years we are going to see that shift, not just for Verdant Works but for mining museums and for any type of industrial museum; we're all experiencing that exact same issue at the moment.'

The visitor experiences that people like Lily can provide is so valuable that conversations around how this can be replicated in the future are ongoing: 'We're looking at a range of things such as trying to pass on knowledge – it would be wonderful to have someone who could come in and learn from Lily, be Lily's apprentice and then that knowledge would be passed on. And the other options are looking at digital. Can we use some of the fantastic technologies that are coming out now?'

One option is targeting new volunteers who have a family connection to the mills. 'We have an oral history project coming up and hopefully we'll recruit people with family connections via the oral history project' explains Oakley. However, thought needs to be given to the different visitor experience that will provide. 'It's a slightly different thing from what we're doing at the moment' she says. 'We'd need to be clear that this was second-hand opinion, as opposed to first hand. You want to make sure the visitor really understands that that's a subtly different story . . . But I think when it comes time to recruit, those might be one of the target demographics that we need to recruit for.'

With such an obvious benefit to the visitor experience from using volunteers with lived experience, how does the Verdant Works team consider what the volunteers themselves get out of their experience? For Oakley, motivations can be different, but in dealing with an older demographic, interaction and socialisation are recurring priorities. Volunteers might jokingly refer to being glad to 'get away' from their spouse, but the truth is more complex than that. 'Not get away from your spouse, but have something to take back to your spouse, so you have something new to talk about' explains Oakley. 'I think that's a really crucial thing. I think a lot of our volunteers get that out of it.'

There are also very altruistic motives at play. 'There's a lot of people who want to give back to society . . . they really want to give back and share' Oakley says. 'We do have people who have a connection to the industry, they worked in the polypropylene industry, or they were an engineer for a short time, those sorts of things . . . and they want to continue to use their skills past retirement.'

As for Lily, volunteering allows her to keep alive the skills and knowledge she has devoted her career to. 'Weaving and working in the industry has been a really big part of her life; it's in her bones, it's what she does. It's really just right through her. So, it allows her to make sure that it doesn't die; it gets kept alive. She's the person who trains the other machine operators; she's trying to pass on her skills and her knowledge.'

CHAPTER 4

Visitor Journey Mapping

> To truly understand the visitor's museum experience, it must be seen as a whole.
>
> (Falk and Dierking, 2016, 174)

Having recruited and trained up your dream team, it's time to turn our attention to the rest of the visitor experience.

Creating a new experience is unlikely to be a solo effort; in museums we work in collaboration to design and deliver every step of the visitor journey. In these early discussions, it's really important to centre the visitor in all decision making. In this chapter, we'll explore one of the best tools we have to do this: the visitor journey map.

Why create a visitor journey map?

Most Visitor Experience professionals will be familiar with the concept of a visitor journey map, and for good reason. It's important for all of us, no matter how big or small our organisation, and regardless of our role within the museum, to take a step back and understand the visitor experience from an outside point of view. Of course, this shouldn't be something that happens just at the start of developing a new experience, so even if you've done this exercise before, it's worth revisiting. Museums are like eco-systems: the smallest change somewhere in the organisation can have a knock-on impact on the visitor offer, and it's good practice to anticipate this before it negatively affects the visitor.

If you haven't been through this process before, it's a simple enough exercise to carry out. Creating a visitor journey map just means sitting down to plan out the touchpoints of your visitor offer, thinking about what you want your visitors to experience at these touchpoints, and then seeing where the gaps in service are. To do this, you'll need two important tools: a clear vision of how you want your visitor experience to look and feel; and an objective sense of what the current reality is (you can find out more about this in Chapter 12, 'Measuring the Visitor Experience').

At the end of this process, you'll have your visitor journey mapped out. You'll have some idea where problems might arise, and you might even know how to fix them. This clarity is exactly why it's important to go through this exercise collaboratively. Even if thinking this stuff through is something you do every day as an operator, other people in the organisation can benefit from coming along on the visitor journey with you. You can use visitor journey mapping as a process to get your team all on the same page, or to convince senior management or trustees of the value of the changes you want to make.

Another reason the process needs to be collaborative is that in larger organisations, a visitor's journey rarely stays within the purview of one department. A visitor might enter through the door staffed by security officers, be greeted by a member of the Visitor Experience team, veer into an exhibition put together by curators, choose a souvenir selected by a retail buyer, then on their way out put some money in a donations box that will later be totted up by somebody in Development. And of course, they'll visit the toilets. Everyone visits the toilets.

Despite this, in many large museums, teams can be focused on function-specific measurements of success, with individual departments never developing a holistic understanding of the visitor journey because some parts of it are simply not in their remit (Kaplan, 2016).

So, whilst it's often the Visitor Experience or Operations teams who will take charge of the journey mapping process, every single museum employee has a stake in and responsibility for the success of that journey. As Falk and Dierking, those stalwarts of museum visitor research, have it: 'to truly understand the visitor's museum experience, it must be seen as a whole' (Falk and Dierking, 2016, 174).

How do we map an experience?

In *Identity and the Museum Visitor Experience*, museum researcher Dr John Falk explains the two lenses traditionally used to understand the visitor experience. The first focuses on the museum; content and programming. For some, this can be the primary or even the only lens. 'The belief that it is all about the content is so pervasive in the museum world that the vast majority, perhaps as much as 90%, of all marketing and promotion of museums is content oriented' (Falk, 2009, 24). The second lens is visitor-focused, with the normal demographics being age, race, gender, socio-economic background, group size, etc.; we're probably all familiar with the usual categories on visitor exit surveys.

In many ways, these traditional lenses still provide value when it comes to understanding our visitors. In a sense, what we are doing with visitor journey mapping is trying to look through both lenses at the same time; understanding what happens when our visitors with their various demographics are placed against the context of our museum.

However, Falk argues that this approach leaves something to be desired: 'We have historically over-focused on either the museum side or visitor side of the equation while neglecting the interaction or the unification of the visitor and the museum into a single unique experience' (Falk, 2009, 34). So, it's not lenses one or two we should be focusing on; it's the dynamic and unpredictable experience that happens when one meets the other. *This* is the unique and hard-to-define phenomenon that we call the visitor experience.

Building visitor profiles

An important part of the visitor journey mapping process is building visitor profiles or personas. These can then be set against our map of touchpoints and help us to understand, from the point of view of the profile or persona, what the visitor experience might look and feel like.

So how can Falk's rejection of traditional visitor demographics help us build better visitor profiles?

Having identified that the key to understanding the visitor experience lies not in understanding the visitor and the museum as separate entities, but in their dynamic interaction, Falk then suggests a model for understanding this new demographic. The idea of 'identity-related visit motivations' or, as Falk explains, 'the series of specific reasons that visitors use to justify as well as organise their visit and ultimately use in order to make sense of their museum experience' (Falk, 2009, 35) is based on extensive research of museum visitors and is, he maintains, key to understanding and predicting visitor expectations.

Simply put, Falk suggests that individuals might be motivated to visit a museum or undertake a cultural activity to reinforce a personal role they identify strongly with. This motivation impacts everything about their visit, including overall satisfaction.

For example, an enthusiast visiting an aircraft museum might measure the success of a visit through how many different aircraft they saw, whether they were able to converse with like-minded enthusiasts, or even whether they had an opportunity to demonstrate their own expertise. These outcomes would reinforce their self-perception of being an aircraft enthusiast, and therefore their personal motivation has been met.

On the other hand, a parent might bring their children to the same museum with the primary motivation of making sure their children have a nice day out. They will measure success by how much this need has been met; did the children have a good time, were the facilities they needed present? (e.g., children's food offering, pocket money items in the shop, children's activities). If these needs are met, the parent will feel that they have made the right decision, and the self-perception that motivated them to choose the museum – the self-perception that they are a good parent – will be reinforced. If the identity-related self-perceptions in either case are not met, the visitor will not feel they have had a satisfactory visit, and will be unlikely to return.

Building on this, Falk categorises visitors into different segments based on their identity-related visit motivations. These categories are set out in Table 4.1.

Table 4.1 *Visitor motivation segments.* Source: Falk, 2009

Facilitator	Might be bringing a family or other group to the museum and is primarily focused on the experience of that group. They may benefit from some structure around this, such as a parents' or kids' guide, and they value experience that places their family or group members centre stage, like interactive demonstrations. Facilitators need spaces and facilities that can host the social encounter they are looking after.
Hobbyist/Professional	Has an expert interest in the subject matter. They value in-depth interactions with professional and knowledgeable staff. They might eschew interpretative tools in favour of their own knowledge, but are likely to be interested in 'behind-the-scenes' content.
Explorer	Explorers are likely to browse and experience a museum in their own way. They are interested in highlights, but may dip in further if their curiosity leads them. Explorers are less likely to use provided interpretative tools, such as guided tours or audio guides; they don't want information spoon-fed.
Recharger	Rechargers use culture to feed their soul and escape from the everyday. They value quiet spaces, seating areas but are least likely to engage with non-exhibit spaces like the café and the shop.
Experience seeker	Interested in experiential culture, one-off experiences and memory making. Interested in seeing the highlights, but need good orientation to make this happen. Value good-quality facilities and great customer service.

I think the model in Table 4.1 stands up, not just because it provides us with a wealth of excellent information with which to build visitor profiles, but because it values all aspects of the museum experience equally (more on this later). However, this isn't to say that other, non identity-related visitor characteristics aren't important or useful for building visitor profiles.

Nick Merriman, for example, cites age and class as strong factors that influence visitor engagement with museums, and explains that this is particularly important when trying to understand people who don't visit museums, along with people who do (Merriman, 2000). These demographics are built into some visitor profile models such as Audience Spectrum from the Audience Agency (2021b), producing a highly detailed segmentation of the UK population that can be very useful when researching the audience for your own organisation.

Like Falk, marketing agency Morris Hargreaves McIntyre (MHM) also looks at motivation in its popular cultural segmentation model. Its approach focuses on people's deep-seated values and beliefs and analyses the impact this has on how they spend their leisure time. It segments visitors into the following categories:

- entertainment
- enrichment
- perspective
- expression
- release
- stimulation
- essence
- affirmation (MHM, 2021)

Although this approach speaks less to the practical aspects of the visitor experience than Falk's, it is hugely useful when developing content experiences and is widely used across the sector.

Other museum writers, such as Paqua and Stewart, remind mappers to focus on visitor emotion, advising the addition of emotional highs and lows to a map so that the whole experience can be measured as a graph (Paqua and Stewart, 2018).

Whilst all of the above approaches (and there are many more) can offer useful inspiration, every museum is different and must build visitor profiles in whichever way works best for them. Some organisations find it useful to personalise; to give profiles names and personalities that bring them to life. Others focus on access needs, using maps to ensure that content is accessible to all, regardless of ability, education, background or language. The most important thing to remember is that, however many profiles you make, every visitor is unique and brings with them a variety of different needs and expectations. You won't be able to predict every single visitor outcome, but hopefully you will be able to anticipate where issues and barriers might arise, and encourage people in your team to deliver flexibility at those critical touchpoints.

It's not just about the exhibits

As hinted at above, I believe that models like the one proposed by Falk are positive in that they dismantle the idea of a hierarchy of museum experiences, with rich content-driven interpretation considered the most impactful, and lowly human needs such as food and bathrooms languishing at the bottom of the tree with little need for thought at all.

In fact, the less obvious factors of a visit can be hugely impactful in shaping the museum experience. For Falk, this all depends on the identity-related visit motivation. For a Facilitator, child-friendly catering facilities might be the difference between a successful museum experience and a disaster, whilst a Hobbyist might not even visit the café. For Falk and Dierking, 'too often neglected are the important notes that some of the less obvious aspects of a visit play in creating the totality of the museum experience' (Falk and Dierking, 2016, 175).

So what are these neglected aspects we should be ensuring are included in our visitor journey maps?

It should be pretty well understood by now that the café or the gift shop can play just as big a role in shaping the visitor experience as the exhibits. True, there are still some in the sector who see them as distractions from the main event, and yet 'in rating the museum experience, the average visitor deems the quality of the gift shops and food service to be as important as, if not more important than, the quality of the artifacts or the exhibition displays' (Falk and Dierking, 2016, 186).

Maybe the reason these areas can feel more out of our control as Visitor Experience professionals is that in larger museums, commercial functions such as the café and the shop might lie with completely different departments, or be subcontracted out entirely. If this is the case in your organisation, don't feel that you can't influence the experience. In creating a visitor journey map, you adopt the view of a visitor; that is to say, you don't worry about which team is in which directorate, or whether the barista might actually work for a different organisation. If the visitor comes into contact with them as part of their overall experience, it's your job to care about it. Part of the benefit of going through the mapping process can often be getting different teams and subcontractors all on the same page and taking equal responsibility for the visitor experience.

Other factors are less departmental and more environmental. If visitors are too hot or too cold, for example, this can have a huge impact on the experience, even curtailing it completely and putting them off a return visit. I remember once being in a meeting where we were discussing the decrease in satisfaction of overseas visitors during the summer months. Marketing colleagues were speculating that their promotion of the summer exhibition must have missed the mark. When we cross-referenced the survey figures with anecdotal feedback, we got the truth: overseas visitors had an expectation that we would have air conditioning. We didn't, and they were too hot.

Other things about the physical environment can have an impact too. It's well known in UK museums, for example, that visitors often turn left when first entering a gallery. Falk and Dierking state that 'visitors will generally exit a gallery through the first door they encounter' (Falk and Dierking, 2016, 133). Unless they are particularly set on a particular route, visitors will often follow the path of least resistance; so, they will go up an escalator, for example, but are less keen to tackle a set of stairs.

All this moving about and going in and out of doors takes its toll, and so another factor museum operators are well aware of is the phenomenon of 'museum fatigue'. Fatigue can have physical but also psychological contributors; the brain can only take in so much, after all. Because of this, it's important to plan resting and recharging into the visitor journey, in particular seating areas and social spaces.

Speaking of the social, visitors rarely experience museums in splendid isolation, so other people form part of that affective environment as well. Large crowds and queues can be a barrier to engagement; on the other hand, other people can influence a visit in positive ways. Connections can be formed; social interactions can be had. Visitors can often use other visitors as templates for behaviour, whether this is negative (for example, dropping litter) or positive (for example, making a donation). Either way, visitors impact each other.

I've already mentioned the one space we can almost guarantee that every visitor will enter: the toilets. These essential rooms have long been underestimated in the museum visit, with many believing that the best they can hope for in this area is clean and functional. Not so, although these two things are very important. Toilets can go a long way to making museum visits easier, and good, accessible or parent-friendly provision is the hallmark of a museum team that have thought about, and indeed care about, their visitors. Toilets can also be social spaces. One of my fondest memories from a visit to the Bilbao Guggenheim is running with my friends through torrential rain to get to the museum, heading to the toilets and photographing our drenched reflections in the mirror with a mixture of amusement and outrage.

Some museums have caught on to the interpretative potential of toilets and brought the museum experience in, so that visitors can carry on engaging with museum content whilst they perform the most essential of human functions. At Hampton Court Palace, for example, six cubicle doors bear the name of Henry VIII's six wives. By entering and turning to face the closed door, visitors can learn the fate of each one. Other bathrooms feature Tudor beauty tips on the walls. There are many other examples, and I love the idea that more care is now being taken to value even the most potentially mundane aspects of a visit as an opportunity for learning.

At the extreme end of the scale, we should remember that museum visitor experiences can be impacted by things we have little or no control over: the journey to the museum, for example, the availability of parking or even the rest of their day. Falk and Dierking explain: 'The museum visit may not even be the first part of the day's experiences; the museum experience might be combined mentally with other things done that day, perhaps other sight-seeing or a breakfast or lunch out' (Falk and Dierking, 2016, 174). Although there may be little we can do to measure or control those impacts, they are certainly worth bearing in mind as part and parcel of the unique needs, expectations and attitudes visitors arrive with.

By considering all of these factors, as well as our more traditional touchpoints such as the welcome, ticketing and the exhibits, we can start to build a truly holistic picture of the visitor journey, and increase our understanding of the different ways visitors can experience our museums.

Taking action

Having introduced visitor journey mapping as a 'simple process', I worry that in writing this chapter I may have thrown so much information and theory at the topic that first-time mappers might be at a loss about where to start.

But the likely truth is that much of what I've described above are things that Visitor Experience professionals already instinctively know. Visitor journey mapping is simply a way to take all of that instinctive knowledge, along with demographic data and visitor feedback, and put it all into a framework that can help you take action to improve your visitor experience:

1 Articulate the vision – what do you want your visitor experience to look like?
2 Describe your visitors – who are they and what are their needs/expectations?

3 Be clear about the current reality at the different touchpoints – what do your visitors say now? What are the issues?
4 Take action – what can you do to improve the situation?

Don't worry about trying to predict every single outcome or possibility. If you can answer these four questions collaboratively and clearly, you'll be well on your way. The key to effective visitor journey mapping isn't in trying to imagine as many pairs of feet as you can, it's in getting every member of your organisation to spend time in shoes other than their own.

Case Study 4: Mail Rail at the Postal Museum

Taking the time to really understand the needs of your audience profiles can be enormously valuable when it comes to trying to make your experience more accessible. A project to do this at the Postal Museum, London, has meant that audiences with different access needs have felt genuinely involved in the co-creation of visitor experiences, but has also led to some surprising outcomes.

One of the big draws at the Postal Museum is the Mail Rail, a train that follows the old track of the underground post trains, and uses digital projection and sound to immerse visitors in a sensory experience. Given the nature of the train, it's not currently accessible for all. There are a number of barriers to access for some audiences. Visitors who are wheelchair users or have significant mobility issues can't ride the train, partially sighted or blind visitors would be unable to experience the visual effects, and those with sensory problems might also find the Mail Rail experience challenging.

When the Postal Museum opened in 2017, an alternative experience known internally as the 'AV bypass' was installed. This allowed people who could not actually travel on the train to sit in a separate booth and watch the audiovisual show. However, Martin Devereaux, Head of Projects and Partnerships at the Postal Museum, describes this experience as 'baseline; the absolute minimum we should be providing' (Devereaux, 2021). Even this 'baseline' experience isn't accessible to all, and whilst it does provide some with an alternative experience, it doesn't provide an equitable experience.

This 'equitable experience' has been the goal of the Postal Museum for some time when it comes to solving the Mail Rail problem, and it's a challenge that is transferable to many other organisations and situations.

When we look at our visitor journey maps from the point of view of a disabled visitor, we need to take action when we find a barrier. So, for example, if we find an entrance is inaccessible to wheelchair users, we might look for an alternative way that user can enter the museum. A different entrance might get them to the same place at the same time; but is it an equitable experience? Coming through the main entrance might be an essential part of the museum experience for a visitor, perhaps a familiar and iconic vista, with every element curated and considered. Does the accessible entrance offer this quality of experience? Would the two visitor journey maps look the same? If not, the secondary entrance may be an alternative to the inaccessible entrance experience, but it's not an equitable one.

In this way, the Postal Museum's 'AV bypass' was a good baseline alternative. It provided a way for visitors to experience the AV show without having to go on the train; but it couldn't match the experience of the train itself and it didn't have the social benefits of going on the ride with friends and family. For this reason, Devereaux explains that as soon as the museum opened, staff were keen to work on a new experience that would (a) be accessible for all and (b) be as much fun as the Mail Rail ride itself.

The Postal Museum team applied for a grant from Innovate UK and worked with a consortium of partners including 3D specialists who had already produced 3D visualisations of the Museum's industrial spaces. The use of these data sets in a virtual reality experience was then explored. Devereaux explains that as these conversations happened, the potential for a truly equitable experience became clear. 'We started thinking that, we could actually do something that in a way that's actually better than the ride. This really allowed you to properly explore Mail Rail, in a way you can't do on the train.'

Mail Rail for All is an ongoing project at the time of writing and the use of 3D technology to produce the perfect accessible experience is still being explored by the Postal Museum. But the real learning from this case study isn't a technological solution that may be out of reach for many small museums, but the design process that has informed the brief.

During a three-month period, the Museum team held several practical workshops with audiences of different abilities: some had mobility issues, some had sensory impairments, others were blind or partially sighted. As well as familiarising the participants with the Museum and the technologies available, 'we got them to talk about their experiences, what they were expecting, what they needed.' It was during these conversations that the team began to understand what would constitute a truly equitable experience for many of the participants: 'They wanted something social. They wanted something that wasn't as isolating as putting goggles on . . . it needs to be more social. And that was the word that came out. Something they could share.'

The process of the workshops also allowed the team to challenge some of their preconceptions about what could and couldn't be achieved. The design process had been very technology-focused, but the needs the participants were expressing were social and experiential. Could these needs be met in a different way? So, while research and development on a technological yet social solution continued, the Museum team began testing another experience in tandem: a tour of Mail Rail for blind and partially sighted people. The train was stopped, and participants were allowed to do something that wouldn't be part of the regular Mail Rail offer – get out of the carriages and explore the track and platform, with one-to-one guiding.

'This was quite revelatory, because first of all it meant that the thing was feasible . . . There are hazards there but with the right mitigations and right processes we can actually facilitate a proper blind and partially sighted tour of the railway tunnels. . . . That was a real success for us, that experience testing, and it wasn't something we'd anticipated from the project. And it shows you that if you do want audiences to be satisfied visitors, then you do have to listen. And yes, it is very resource intensive, you've got to have the staff, the staff have to be trained, you have to effectively take the train out of commission, so it does disrupt your normal operating model, but it's probably worth it when all is said and done, because the kind of benefits you reap in terms of customer satisfaction, engagement with your audiences; that has such a long tail to it afterwards.'

So whilst the perfect technological solution remains a work in progress, the workshops have allowed the team to refine the design brief. The experience had to be accessible for all, any sort of viewing experience had to be a shared one, and importantly, it included the idea that the best way of making connections between audiences and the museum 'is always through people' (Devereaux, 2021). In addition, the collaborative work done with the workshop participants has inspired a greater understanding of what visitors want, and the subsequent development of a whole new experience completely divorced from the technological solution that had been anticipated.

What practical advice can Devereaux give to museums looking to build visitor profiles through a similar process?

1. Listen to your audiences; don't predict what they might want.
2. When experience planning, think about how people with different access needs can do things together. Don't compartmentalise; in real life they won't be in working groups.
3. If people have access issues, they will bring these access issues to the workshops. So, think about transportation and facilitation and budget carefully.
4. Invest in the personal: the best connection between the audience and the museum will always be via people.

Ultimately, developing and using visitor profiles works best when there is real collaboration between the audiences and the museum. As Devereaux says: 'it's not just dictating to them the kind of experience we want to give them, but working with them to explore options and make suggestions and using that to shape the project.'

CHAPTER 5
Ticketing, Capacities and Crowd Management

> I am not sure how we managed to work before these new systems!
>
> (Steven Jugg, The Stained-Glass Museum)

Although there are an increasing number of virtual museums these days, most of the museums we work in remain bricks-and-mortar buildings. There are, of course, lots of advantages to this: for many heritage sites, the bricks-and-mortar and what once happened within them is the whole point of the visitor experience! But a physical building brings with it physical limitations. Many heritage sites were never designed, in form nor fabric, to welcome large numbers of visitors per year. Even in the largest, newest sites there is a finite capacity to the volume of people we can host.

These limitations have led to the development of an entire science devoted to how we can best manage capacity in our museums. The world of ticketing systems, pre-booking technology, and crowd management can often feel like a slightly intimidating body of water; deep, unfathomable and often murky. But it's well worth diving into, because applying just a few visitor management techniques could streamline the overall experience and make on-site processes much easier for your teams. In this chapter, we'll take a look at some of these techniques and how they can make for a smoother, richer and above all safer visitor experience.

Capacity management

The first step to capacity management is knowing what the capacity is. There are a few different factors that might influence this. The first and more important will be the fire capacity. This is the number that the Fire Risk Assessment for your building says you are legally permitted to have in the building at any one time. It should take into account things like the activity undertaken by visitors (will people be standing or sitting, dancing or walking, eating or drinking alcohol?) and the number of fire exits, stairs, internal corridors, etc. Your Fire Risk Assessment is a critical document, so if the museum doesn't have the in-house resource such as a Fire Officer to carry it out, it's important to seek outside assistance from a consultant.

It's critical to never exceed your fire capacity number, and you may well find that if you are looking for the *comfort* capacity of your building, you might need to lower it. This is because a fire capacity could assume that visitors will be perfectly spaced out across the museum; and we all know visitors don't work like that. For example, when I worked at the Natural History Museum, most visitors congregated in the Dinosaur Gallery and Central Hall area, and were far less prevalent in other parts of the Museum. So, we had a fire capacity of 11,000, but a comfort capacity closer to 5,500.

Senior Marketing Manager at Gateway, Greg Banecker, advises concentrating on the busiest areas when calculating capacity. 'Focus on key congestion areas and work up from there. What percentage of your guests are in that area at any given time? . . . Then do the math from there' (Banecker, 2020).

Another key element in the equation is dwell time. If your capacity is 5,500, it doesn't mean you can only welcome 5,500 people a day: it all depends on how long they spend on site. Knowing this means you can start to think about ticketing your experience. For example, for sites with a long dwell time, a morning or afternoon admission ticket might be offered. For sites with a shorter dwell time, tickets can be sold for each hour or half hour timeslot, with capacity reached not in one timeslot but by the cumulative total of people on site at any one time. This approach offers flexibility as well; as long as capacity hasn't been breached, visitors who arrive early or late, or those who have walked up without a ticket, can be accommodated.

The last part in the equation is knowing your out-count as well as your in-count. Even if you have an idea of the average dwell time, you need to be sure of exactly how many people are on site at any one time; this means subtracting the number of people who have left that day from the number of people who have arrived. Many museums do this with technology; whether low-tech, such as turnstiles or turnbars, or more high-tech options like ticket scanning or infrared people counters. Or, as Banecker suggests, 'just make sure you have a good old-fashioned human monitoring exit scans in some way and sharing that data with your team' (Banecker, 2020).

Data is important, because once you have some good evidence as to how visitors are using your museum, you can start to tweak accordingly. I would always start with a low-capacity number when launching a new experience: it's easier to add more capacity than take it away!

Some of you might work in museums where capacities are never reached and therefore, these are sums that are simply not worth doing. However, things can change quickly. In 2020 and 2021 the capacities of museums, large and small, were dramatically impacted by COVID-19. This is a good example of why it's worth bearing in mind that there will always be new challenges that affect how we manage people; and our perception of 'comfort' capacities could continue to fluctuate for reasons beyond our control.

Managing crowds

For many museums, capacities are reached regularly and so crowd management is an essential part of the visitor operation. Other museums may not have to deal with crowds on a regular basis, but remember: it's all dependent on relative size, space and staffing. In a small museum with few entrances and exits and limited staff resource, even a small group of people can become an unmanageable crowd surprisingly quickly. Therefore, it's well worth incorporating some crowd management theory into your visitor management plans.

I've always thought that the term 'crowd management' tends to come with negative connotations, probably because we hear it most associated with news stories about crowd disasters. It sounds like we're trying to solve a problem. It sounds like we would have a lot easier job if the crowds just went away. However, when the COVID-19 pandemic hit in 2020, we all experienced what it was like to lose our crowds; and I don't think many of us were hoping it would remain a permanent situation!

I think crowd management should be something that we want to be doing. It shouldn't be a case of working against the crowd, or trying to get rid of the crowd, it should be a case of working with the people in the crowd to safely deliver the experiences we all want to have.

Crowd management is important because we've all seen examples of the tragedies that can occur when it goes wrong. In those news stories we might have read, it's unfortunately far too common for the people hurt in crowd disasters to be blamed for the loss of life, as happened after the Hajj crush in 2015 and in the UK, the Hillsborough disaster in 1989. However, this blame is misplaced, as we've seen with the Hillsborough enquiry here in the UK (Conn, 2019). Experts believe the failures that lead to most tragedies are at a management rather than an individual level (Benedictus, 2015).

Management failings can be things like lack of staff resource, lack of available exits, over-selling or booking tickets, lack of staff training and poor communication; all issues that can crop up in the museum context as well as sports arenas. It's important for crowd managers to look at previous crowd disasters to learn how those management issues arise. In fact, in the UK much of our crowd management legislation and guidance is based on previous fatal disasters such as Hillsborough and the Ibrox stadium crowd crush in 1971, which is why it has the rather macabre nickname of 'tombstone legislation'.

Because 'tombstone legislation' has been shaped by historic disasters, in the UK that means most guidance relates to music and sporting events. There are currently two main published pieces of crowd management guidance, colloquially referred to as the Green Guide and the Purple Guide. The Green Guide (https://sgsa.org.uk/greenguide) is guidance for sporting events and the Purple Guide (https://thepurpleguide.co.uk) is for music events and festivals. Neither is specifically aimed at visitor attractions, so we have to adapt that guidance to best fit our needs. Once you've done that, using those guides as the basis for your crowd management plans can help you work out some of the practical elements, such as the recommended number of staff members to visitors. But if you're dealing with high-volume crowds in your museum, you also need to consider those management issues I mentioned above, such as training and communication.

The most important issue to consider is whether you will be able to safely evacuate your crowded museum in an emergency. This, of course, is a huge topic, and if you manage a museum where you regularly deal with large crowds, I would strongly recommend an in-depth crowd management course; there are many good suppliers and options out there. In the meantime, here are just a few things to consider.

The main problems with crowd evacuations come from the practicalities of the situation itself rather than individual behaviour. The more people there are, the more likely it is that something dangerous will happen, and that there will be more potential victims. Communication can be hard in crowded places, due to noise, number of people and the distances concerned. It can also be harder to move around, due to people having conflicting destinations and not much room to move in. Then, if a space is evacuated, you are faced with a lot of people trying to go to one exit quickly, as people will often be drawn to exit the same way they came in.

These are all issues that can be planned for:

- Any public building should have multiple fire exits (how many will depend on your Fire Risk Assessment – or in older buildings, your capacity will be determined by how many fire exits you do have), and staff should be trained to actively evacuate people through lots of different exit options as opposed to just the main entrance.
- In large attractions, you should ensure someone is monitoring an evacuation from a CCTV or control room. This way, they can issue live directive messages via radio if bottlenecks are starting to appear.

- Clear communication is critical. Fire or emergency alarms that issue a tone or a noise rather than words rarely work alone, and even with a verbal alarm, the role of staff in managing the evacuation on the ground couldn't be more important.
- Panicking, fleeing visitors are rarely the problem in a crowd evacuation; it's more likely to be getting people to evacuate at all. Many visitors are used to false alarms, and they can be unwilling to leave the building, especially if they have queued to get in, or they have just sat down with a lovely cake and coffee in the café. So, staff have to be polite, but assertive; urgent, but calm. It's important to reiterate to staff that their responsibility to visitors ends at firm advice; they can't force people to leave, and should never put themselves at risk to do so.
- Live training exercises are a must, to help staff build the key phrases, skills and confidence they will need in a real emergency.

Even in non-emergency situations, crowds and queues can be problematic for museums. As operators, we're always delighted to know that our museums are popular, but there's no denying that crowds can cause barriers to some visitors, particularly those with access needs, families with young children or even just visitors with limited time in their day (Mackay, 2021). So, how can we mitigate some of these barriers in our museums?

Pre-booking

In 2020, COVID-19 threw pre-booking dramatically into the spotlight, and yet it has been on the agenda of many museums for a long time. This is because the benefits of such a system are many and varied.

For museum operations teams, advanced booking means we have a much better idea of how busy our sites are likely to be on any given day, and can plan our resources accordingly. It means visitors are more likely to turn up. In fact, a 2020 research study by BVA BDRC showed that 11% of those surveyed had followed through on a visit purely because they had pre-booked (Young, 2020). For outdoor attractions, where visit motivation can be heavily impacted by weather, this is a potential game changer. Pre-booking also allows attractions to spread their visitor load more evenly across the day, meaning that groups are more manageable for staff, queues are shorter and the resulting on-site experience is more enjoyable for visitors. There are also many commercial advantages to pre-booking, which I'll discuss in more detail below.

For free museums, or attractions with a high number of free member visits, the biggest problem with pre-booking over 2020 and 2021 has been visitors booking and then not turning up: 'no-shows'. The same BVA BDRC study found that for some attractions, 'no-shows' had been as high as 30%, although Research Director Jon Young adds: 'The truer number is likely to be higher – even in a survey environment people will feel bad about sharing undesirable behaviour.'

Young suggests some ways to reduce the 'no-show' phenomenon, including plenty of reminders leading up to the booking and the use of flexible booking software: 'Some – like the Roman Baths – allow you to cancel your visit up to the last minute. Others don't allow cancellation at all. It's no surprise, therefore, that the likes of the Roman Baths have comparatively low "no-show" rates – although the price point will also be a driver.'

What, then, has the great COVID-19 ticketing experiment taught us about the future of pre-booking? In the survey, three out of four people said they thought 100% pre-booking post-COVID-19 was a good thing. This is encouraging, but it's clear that pre-booking remains a barrier for some, including the casual, spontaneous visitor, whilst also potentially excluding some key audiences, such as international visitors and older people (Young, 2020).

It seems clear that where possible, museums should be aiming for a mixed model to best ensure that all audiences are able to access our visitor offers. Hitting on the right pre-book/walk-up capacity is a matter for each individual museum: it all depends on who your audience is, where they travel from, and how long they spend with you. I would advocate a programme of trial and test before settling on the right figure. For free museums, trial and test will also help identify average 'no-show' percentages, allowing you to 'over-book' capacities and ensure you are not wasting any tickets.

Choosing the right ticketing system

To manage capacities, admissions and pre-booking, the most critical piece of technology you invest in will be the right ticketing system.

The ticketing landscape has changed beyond recognition in the last decade. In times gone by the main concern with a ticketing system would be the hardware costs and where to space your till points. The advent of cloud-based options, progress in allowing systems to run on off-the-shelf hardware like iPads and the improvement of networks across attractions has changed the way we now plan ticketing projects. It has also brought ticketing software within reach of many smaller attractions that would traditionally have relied on in-person sales and cash handling.

It's not just admission sales that have seen a huge transformation in recent years. A good EPOS system (electronic point of sale) alongside a good webstore (the part of your system that will deal with online sales) can deliver so much for your museum, including live capacity management, gift aid, donations, cross-selling and upselling and of course, give you lots of useful data on who your visitors are. It's a massive area, so before embarking on refreshing your ticketing approach, I would advise putting together a list of your current requirements, as well as thinking seriously how ticketing can support the growth of your museum in the future.

This list of requirements will help you narrow down the incredibly wide field of ticketing suppliers out there, and it's important to do a thorough comparison of the market. As consultant Nick Kime advises on the Museums Association website: 'Finding the system that meets your functionality requirements and budget is vital, so it is important you explore a wide spectrum of systems to ensure you select the right product for you' (Kime, 2020).

Be wary of ticketing suppliers offering to develop future products or functionality further down the line. Salespeople have been known to over-promise and if you are keen to avoid under-delivery, make your decision based on what they can offer straight out of the box, rather than a vision of a fantasy future!

Once a supplier has been chosen, one of the most significant barriers to successfully implementing a new system can be lack of engagement or training in the user team. A change in systems can a be a big hurdle for some teams, especially if they work infrequently (e.g., on seasonal or casual contracts) or if the museum is reliant on volunteers. In these situations, Kime recommends 'creating digital champions in your organisation who have a natural affinity for using the software and task them with spreading positivity and knowledge of the system to others'. Some suppliers can also assist with on-site implementation, working hand-in-hand with till operators and other stakeholders to ensure the system is fully embedded and helping to iron out any teething issues. If you think this would be useful for your team, make sure you know up front whether this is something your preferred supplier would offer as part of their contract.

Generating income

The ability to pre-book tickets offers many opportunities for income generation as well as effective capacity management.

The information you get from visitors prior to their arrival is important not just for resource planning, but for knowing where and how to target commercial activity in the future. It also allows you to start building a relationship with visitors before they even arrive on site. There are great visitor experience benefits here, for example in sending through digital content to get them excited about their visit, as well as upselling opportunities. For example, as ticketing consultant Carly Straughan suggests, how about 'an activity pack for the kids to complete before they get to visit in real life or a book about the founders of your museum' (Straughan, 2021)? With pre-visit retail, Straughan advises museums to 'steer away from generic items and really showcase what your site is famous for to encourage people to spend with you.'

There are also opportunities in pre-visit catering spend. Pre-booking catering before arriving on site can help visitors in a variety of ways, from the peace of mind of knowing that specific dietary requirements can be catered for to offering the luxury of a fine-dining experience. Spending this money beforehand doesn't mean that visitors won't spend on site. In fact, Straughan says 'it's proven that by removing the purchase from the day of the visit most visitors will spend more when they are physically on site with you.'

It isn't just the museum that can benefit financially from pre-booking: many sites offer a good discount on early online booking, so often the visitor can benefit too.

Therefore, with a bit of thought and investment, the challenges of capacity management and crowding can often be utilised to provide a better visitor experience for your guests and a smoother operation for your teams.

Case Study 5: A new approach to ticketing at the Stained-Glass Museum

The Stained-Glass Museum can be found inside Ely Cathedral, and houses a collection spanning over 800 years of stained-glass art. In 2020, during the COVID-19 closures, the Museum staff took the opportunity to use Cultural Recovery Fund (set up by the UK Government to support cultural recovery after the COVID-19 pandemic) money to take a deep dive into their online ticketing and sales processes and see how they could provide a better visitor experience going forward.

Shop and Visitor Services Manager Steven Jugg describes the situation at the Stained-Glass Museum prior to this work: 'Our previous working system was an old-fashioned till that allowed us to record sales by categories and record visitor numbers but then needed to be manually entered into multiple spreadsheets for daily, monthly, annual totals and analysis. The system did not allow us to track, monitor or review stock easily. There were often problems with hand-transferring data, with no system tracking your process it was hard to pinpoint the problem. We did not have a centralised system for selling tickets online and most of our admission and event ticket sales were taken in person or over the phone and entered into spreadsheets' (Jugg, 2022).

The Stained-Glass Museum team worked with Carly Straughan at Q-LINE Consulting to scope a new ticketing and retail system. Much of this work was developing a detailed understanding of what was needed. The Stained-Glass Museum is a relatively small attraction, welcoming approximately 9,000 visitors per year. Some of the all-singing, all-dancing systems were therefore too much for the Museum team's requirements, or simply out of their budget. The focus was on finding system support that could simply and easily modernise the Museum's processes whilst also opening up more income generation opportunities and providing a smooth visitor experience.

Straughan explains: 'Initially, we worked out what the museum needed us to do. We visited and talked to people at different stages of both the visitor experience and behind the scenes organisation. This included admissions, stock management and e-commerce' (Q-LINE, 2022). The research was the most important part of the process. Straughan created a detailed Request for Proposal (RFP) based on the Museum's requirements and created a report analysing the long list of respondents before whittling it down to a shortlist with demonstrations and requests for more information.

Q-LINE recommended two cloud-based systems for the Stained-Glass Museum. The first was Art Tickets, which is available as a free service to Art Fund members. Art Fund don't charge for credit card processing, and there is no ongoing contract, so it is an easy, low-risk option for smaller museums. The Stained-Glass Museum can now sell tickets online, including pre-booking for workshops, children's activities and talks. Whilst it may not have the functionality of the more expensive ticketing systems, for the museum it was 'the most appropriate one (within budget and thinking of ease of use/long-term affordability)' (Q-LINE, 2022).

Shopify, a cloud-based retail POS, was chosen for similar reasons. Not only is Shopify easy to use, it comes with a variety of different pricing plans, so you can tailor the level of functionality to your budget. Again, there was no ongoing contract, and it came with great, contemporary hardware options. For the Stained-Glass Museum, it meant easy training of new staff and 'improving stock management accuracy which was previously done manually' (Q-LINE, 2022).

Jugg says 'I am not sure how we managed to work before these new systems; they have helped us streamline and centralise payments and bookings and improved the customer experience immensely, freeing up time for our staff to focus on visitors.'

This case study demonstrates that putting in systems that dramatically change your ticketing experience don't have to cost the earth. It's all about getting a good understanding of your needs and requirements, and choosing the right system for you.

PART 2

Managing the Visitor Experience

In the second part of this book, we will move into examining the real meat of delivering the visitor experience: the day-to-day management of an operation and a team.

In Chapter 6, we examine the procedures we use to manage an operation and the all-important role of the Duty Manager. I'll suggest some best practice, and a case study from world-class heritage attraction Stonehenge will show how service recovery can turn a situation round even when things go wrong.

Chapter 7 will explore the most important role of the Visitor Experience Manager: managing a team. We'll look at motivation and performance management, both good and not so good.

In Chapter 8, I'll use a case study from a previous role at Kew Palace to further explore how we look after our teams. In this instance, I will focus on the emotional wellbeing of our teams, and specifically, what we can do to safeguard this when dealing with exhibitions, collections and programmes that include challenging content.

Chapter 9 deals with that mainstay of museum visitor experience: the guided tour. We'll look at the pros and cons of guided tours and use a case study from the highly successful Hidden London tours from the London Transport Museum to explore best practice.

Finally, we'll look at what happens when that day-to-day management goes straight out of the window! Crisis management practice has been heavily impacted by the experience of COVID-19, so Chapter 10 reviews our learnings and suggests new best practice for keeping our crisis management plans and processes ready to go.

CHAPTER 6

Operational Procedures

> I imagine your worst day out and try to stop it from happening.
>
> (David Hingley, Tate)

This is the chapter that I would probably refer to as the 'bread and butter' of operations. As much as we Visitor Experience professionals devote our time to making museum trips the absolute best they can be, it's inevitable that our roles can often be defined by what happens when something goes wrong. This is neatly summed up by the words at the start of this chapter, from the Twitter bio of a former colleague of mine, David Hingley. A great Duty Manager shift is when the building *doesn't* set on fire, when the tills *don't* go down, when a staff member *isn't* shouted at by an angry visitor.

In operations, though our successes are signalled more by silence than fireworks, we shouldn't underestimate the amount of work it takes to achieve relative calm. Like the swan gliding effortlessly across a pond, beneath the surface our legs are thrashing energetically through a never-ending slew of risk assessments, training modules and standard operating procedures (SOPs). To do this effectively, one needs a good understanding of the audience, a great relationship with frontline teams, an unhealthy attention to detail and most importantly, a deeply morbid imagination.

A Visitor Experience Manager might be asked to create a suite of operational procedures from scratch, but more often, procedures are already in place. They have built up over years of organisational memory, made up of incidents that have occurred and questions people have asked. They are built on good solid experience but, nevertheless, it's important to review these procedures every so often (at least once a year) to make sure they are still fit for purpose. Whether you are creating operational procedures for a brand-new offer, or just conducting a regular health check of your existing ones, hopefully this chapter will give you some practical tips around best practice, training and structure.

Before I talk about specific operational incidents, it's worth spending some time on the context in which operational management occurs.

The Duty Manager

There are probably as many operational management structures as there are museums. Each has its own strengths and, of course, you'll need to think about what structure works best for your organisation.

One of the most important roles in Operations is that of the Duty Manager. This could be one designated person, or in bigger museums, it could be a rotating role that different managers take on at different times.

Collins English Dictionary defines a Duty Manager as 'a person who is in charge at a particular time' (Collins Dictionary, 2021). Although the scope of a museum Duty Manager can vary, generally they are the person responsible for the daily operation of the museum, from the moment the doors open till the last visitor leaves at the end of the day. As such, they direct the whole operational team, even if they aren't under their specific line management. They will be the first point of contact for any incidents, and they will play a crucial role in an emergency. Here are some examples of tasks that might fall under the responsibility of the Duty Manager:

- opening and closing the museum doors
- cashing up
- responding to visitor complaints
- service recovery
- dealing with unattended items
- ensuring the museum is safe to open
- liaising with emergency services if required
- managing the capacity of the museum.

However, there will likely be a hundred other things that a Duty Manager ends up doing every day; whatever it takes to keep the museum running smoothly.

In small museums, the Duty Manager might end up covering other duties, particularly front of house. This is fine if it's quiet, but being pinned to specific duties like the front desk leaves you unable to respond to incidents elsewhere in the museum. In a sustainable management structure, the Duty Manager should be free to swoop in where needed to offer targeted support.

In larger museums where the duty management function is rotated, it's really important to have consistency so that communication and standards are clear. For example, you might answer to 'Duty Manager' on the radio and use a specific Duty Manager mobile rather than your own communication channels. I've found it helpful in the past to chair regular Duty Manager meetings and implement a Duty Manager development programme to ensure everyone is on the same page, no matter what department they are based in.

It's also key for a Duty Manager team to be able to pass daily information to each other. In some cases, this can be as simple as writing a handover note, but if the Duty Manager also has a reporting function (for example, sending round daily visitor figures, or reporting maintenance defects), it might be easier to combine the two things into a daily Duty Management report that can be accessed by all.

Across all museums, the Duty Manager is a floor-focused role, not a desk job. They should be a highly visible point of contact, ready to deal with any incidents, offer support where needed and ensure services standards are kept high throughout the whole visitor operation.

In much larger museums, the structure might be even more complex. For example, when I worked at the Natural History Museum, we had both a Duty Manager and a Site Manager. The Duty Manager looked after the daily operation, but the Site Manager was a more senior role that could step in and assist with any emergency situations, such as evacuations, and was also there as a sounding board if the Duty Manager needed any advice or support. As a Duty Manager, you would manage an evacuation from the floor, whereas the Site Manager would go to the control room and be able to provide a more strategic overview using the CCTV.

This roughly coincides with the Bronze and Silver emergency command positions used by the emergency services, and although these separate levels will only really be necessary for the largest size of museums, it's important to know that the structure you have in place could deliver the emergency plan if needed.

Culture and context

Before moving on to the typical operational incidents, I think it's important to make the point that the culture inside which the incidents are handled is as important as the incident itself, as Figure 6.1 on the next page illustrates.

Imagine the incident not as an isolated occurrence, but surrounded by layers of meaning that can affect it in different ways. The first layer is the direct behaviour of the staff and visitors involved in the incident. Obviously, this can impact the incident in a number of ways. Around that, we have organisational structures. These are the procedures and policies put in place by the museum, both to prevent incidents from occurring e.g. risk assessments and staff training, and to deal with them when they do happen,

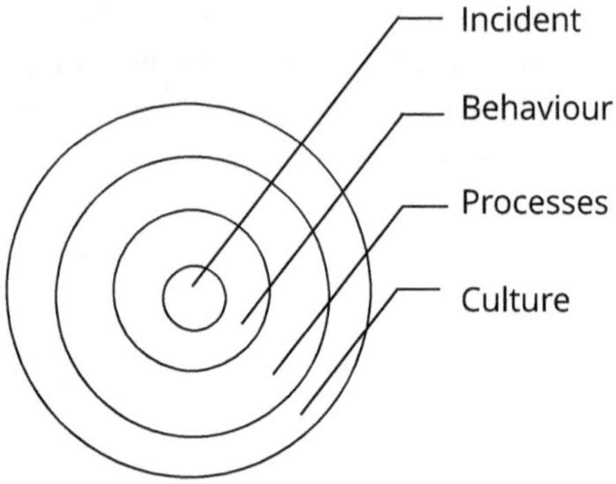

Figure 6.1 *Organisational culture of incidents*

such as standard operating procedures. But even those are affected by the outermost layer: the organisational culture.

Fostering a culture that supports effective incident management is critical to each individual element. A supportive culture in this regard might have some or ideally all of the following features:

- wash-ups of incidents so lessons can be learned in a blame-free environment
- planning and looking to try to predict flashpoints or negative reactions
- regular and ongoing staff training and development
- clear communication channels
- high levels of autonomy for front-facing staff
- managers who support and encourage staff decision making on the floor
- 360-degree feedback.

If there are gaps in this list when it comes to your organisation, long-term effective incident management will be hard to implement.

Operational incidents

As mentioned above, every organisation is different and has different requirements when it comes to operational incident management. However, whether you are starting from scratch or merely refreshing your processes, you may find some pointers around best practice to be helpful. Table 6.1 opposite is a list of the most common operational procedures, along with some helpful tips to consider when planning procedures. I've also outlined some further reading so that UK organisations can reference the appropriate legislation (at time of writing).

Table 6.1 *Things to consider in operational incidents*

Incident	Important things to consider	Find out more
Lost child or vulnerable adult	• From a Safeguarding perspective, ensure that lost children are never left alone with a staff member. If this is unavoidable, staff should go through appropriate security checking. • Find an appropriate location to co-ordinate any lost child enquiries. Parents/carers will usually gravitate naturally to an entrance or reception desk if they are looking for help. • The priority when looking for a lost child or vulnerable adult is to have eyes on your external boundary, so you can concentrate on searching internal areas without worrying that they have wandered off or been taken off site. • Make sure the parent/carer knows what your search procedure is and can see it in action. For example, if you co-ordinate a search of your galleries, make sure every member of staff vocally reports back (via radio, for example) even if they haven't found anything. This gives the parents/ carers reassurance that action is being taken. • How long would you look for the lost person before involving the police? This can be based on many factors: rural or urban environment, presence or otherwise of water, busy roads, ease of penetration of the external boundary, vulnerability of lost person etc. • Always make sure you have confirmation that the incident has ended. Keep the parent/carer with you, otherwise they might find their lost person and you might not be any the wiser.	Links to official UK Government law and guidance around safeguarding can be found here: www.gov.uk/government/publications/working-together-to-safeguard-children—2
Evacuation	• Fire evacuation procedures should be prepared in conjunction with the Fire Safety Officer, based on a Fire Risk Assessment of the building. Responsibilities for monitoring the fire system, responding to activations and calling the fire brigade should be clearly stated and appropriate training given. • Be aware that there may be other issues for evacuation, such as bomb threats or power failure. In some of these circumstances, you may need to plan for a 'silent evacuation'.	Official UK Government guidance on evacuation plans for small and medium places of assembly can be found here: https://assets.publishing.service.gov.uk/government/uploads/system/uploads/attachment_data/file/973794/9294_Small_Mediumt_v2.pdf

Continued

Table 6.1 *Continued*

Incident	Important things to consider	Find out more
	• Radios are critical in evacuating large spaces. Ensure teams are trained in the correct procedures including maintaining radio silence during emergencies except for critical information. • Evacuations should be regularly and rigorously rehearsed through frequent fire drills.	
Invacuation	• An invacuation would occur when you have public outside your building and want to get them inside away from danger. • These situations can be extremely dynamic and call for quick decision making, e.g. whether to invacuate and risk bringing a threat inside the museum space (for example if there has been a terror incident on the street). • Developing critical thinking skills in the operational management team is therefore essential for planning for these incidents.	Official UK Government advice on planning for invacuation can be found here: www.gov.uk/government/publications/crowded-places-guidance/evacuation-invacuation-lockdown-protected-spaces
Lost property	• Have a clear policy on lost property, including how long items are retained for, and stick to it. • Ensure any high-value items (phones, credit cards etc.) are removed from the floor or front desk as soon as possible and secured by a manager. • Always be mindful of handling personal data when you are dealing with lost property, particularly in regard to credit cards and passports, etc.	Official UK Government guidance on GDPR can be found here: www.gov.uk/government/publications/guide-to-the-general-data-protection-regulation
Potentially violent situation (PVS)	• This could include a variety of incidents including protest action, abuse towards staff or visitors, vandalism or inappropriate attention to children or others. Basically, if a member of staff ever feels that they can't handle a situation, or that they, a colleague or a visitor may be in danger, it's a PVS. • In some cases (for example when face to face with an angry visitor) it may be useful to have a code word to use over the radio to avoid exacerbating the situation. • A member of staff should never face criticism for calling for support for a PVS, even if as a manager you feel it was unwarranted. If they feel at risk, then they are.	Office UK Government guidance on what training is needed to hold a Security Industry Authority (SIA) licence can be found here: www.gov.uk/guidance/check-what-training-you-need-to-get-an-sia-licence A short online summary of conflict resolution training can be found here: www.therecoveryroomblog.com/conflict-resolution

Continued

Table 6.1 *Continued*

Incident	Important things to consider	Find out more
	• Be mindful of who attends a report of a PVS. It might be useful to prescribe this beforehand in larger museums. You might want a security back-up, for example, but if you specifically plan for who that will be (e.g. the Duty Security Officer) you avoid every security officer in the building turning up, which again, may exacerbate things. Security officers should take the lead on any action such as restraining or ejecting individuals, as they will have had the appropriate training to do so. • It's important to check in with everyone involved in a PVS afterwards to make sure everyone is okay and understands why decisions were made. • Investing in some good conflict resolution training will make a PVS easier to manage and hopefully quicker to resolve – as well as giving frontline staff more confidence that they can deal with any incidents.	
Lift trapping	• When planning for lift trappings, ensure you have up-to-date information about response times from your lift contractor. • If your lift contractor can't respond within a reasonable time or at weekends, your only back-up is to call the fire brigade. If this happens often you will eventually be charged, so aim to influence any contract negotiations toward ensuring weekend call-outs are covered! • Lifts should be checked and serviced regularly. • Always check in advance with your lift contractor or manufacturer about what to do during and after a power cut or a long period out of use. • Never attempt lift repairs yourself.	Official UK Health and Safety Executive advice on the use of lifts can be found here: www.hse.gov.uk/work-equipment-machinery/passenger-lifts.htm
First aid	• There is no legal necessity for you to have first aiders for visitors; however, it is legally necessary to have them for your staff. • Saying that, having first aid provision for visitors is good practice, has come to be an expectation of visitors, and most importantly, could save lives. • It's important to keep accurate records about first aid training and refresher courses, number of first aiders and supply of first aid materials.	Official UK Health and Safety Executive advice on first aid at work can be found here: www.hse.gov.uk/firstaid

Continued

Table 6.1 *Continued*

Incident	Important things to consider	Find out more
	• Availability of a defibrillator can be critical. Ensure your staff know where your nearest one is, and if you have your own one, make sure it is checked regularly. It's certainly worth investing in this if you have an area that is higher-risk for certain visitors e.g. a steep climb. • Always check in with first aiders after incidents – they can be traumatic. • Ensure staff know they should not attempt to deliver first aid unless they have a current first aid qualification that has been recorded and recognised by the museum. • If an ambulance needs to be called, make sure this is always co-ordinated through the same channels to avoid confusion. Usually this would be done either by the Duty Manager or the museum's control room.	
Unattended item	• Any unattended item should be treated as a threat until found to be otherwise. • Train staff in HOT procedures (Hidden, Obvious, Typical) to ensure threats are quickly spotted. • Don't use radios in the immediate vicinity of an unattended item as this can affect radio-controlled explosive devices. • When clearing areas around a suspect package, bear in mind official advice in regard to evacuation distances: 'Take charge and move people away to a safe distance. Even for a small item such as a briefcase move at least 100m away from the item' (Protect UK, 2022).	Protect UK guidance on unattended items, including information on the HOT principles, can be found here: www.protectuk.police.uk/incident-procedures

Standard operating procedures (SOPS)

When I started my first Duty Manager role I had no idea what a SOP was. Everyone kept talking about them, and before long it had passed the point where I could reasonably ask what on earth they were going on about. Anyway, I found out eventually – SOP stands for 'standard operating procedure' and the reason they came up so much in conversation is that they are an essential part of the daily work of the museum operations team.

SOPs are standalone documents that succinctly outline the agreed processes for dealing with a particular incident or event. Like a risk assessment, they usually have an owner and a review date, meaning they are living documents that should be updated frequently. SOPs do no good at all sitting on a computer drive; they should be something that you interact with on a regular basis.

SOPs have several uses. In writing them, you think through the issues and solve problems. Not only that, but if you're working collaboratively, a consensus should be created that means all the operational team are on the same page when it comes to dealing with that specific issue. They are also useful for training new team members, or for refreshing memories, for example if you have a seasonal operation. Finally, they are critical documents when dealing with any visitor complaints or claims: by producing them, you show that you have an agreed-upon process for dealing with things and aren't making it up as you go along.

Every museum has a different format (or even different name) for SOPs, but if this is something you haven't seen before, I've included an example in Figure 6.2 on the next page.

Training and engagement

The most important factor in planning to deal with operational incidents is staff training and engagement.

Training in operational incidents can be tricky, as most of it falls under the banner of 'Health and Safety' and eyes can often begin to glaze over, particularly if the training is coming during a long induction period. To ensure good engagement, it's important to keep operational training:

- relevant – staff should understand WHY this stuff is so important
- practical – operational procedures are best learned by DOING
- ongoing – operational excellence comes from regular PRACTICE.

The best way to make operational training relevant is by ensuring that staff know about the kinds of things that are most likely to happen to them on the museum floor. This can happen through existing staff sharing stories, new staff talking about incidents that have happened in previous roles, or for the more serious incidents, looking at incidents that have made the headlines. I like to get teams to think about how they would react to similar incidents and the impact it could have on their lives and others. This helps the possibility of operational incidents and the importance of their response feel more real.

Much of this training is best done as practically as possible. Role play can be used to great effect for conflict resolution training, especially when exploring different interactions and scenarios (Mackay, 2020a). If you are training on dealing with unattended items, a practical solution can be to make

ORGANISATION NAME
Standard Operating Procedure: Power Cuts
Owner: Rachel Mackay
Last Updated: XX XX XXXX
Introduction
This document describes the standard operating procedures for dealing with power cuts.
Duty Manager will decide if a Silent Evacuation is necessary for these incidents.
Power Cut/Failure
In the event of a prolonged power failure, emergency lighting will automatically activate and last 15 minutes. The Duty Manager will start a silent evacuation if the public are in the building. The emergency lighting is a means of escape only.
Power failure may be due to the loss of supply from the electrical provider or due to a fault in the palace electrical systems. The Duty Manager should contact the control room and establish if the failure is local to the museum or general to the site.

- In the event of a local loss, the Duty Manager should contact the control room and request the duty electrician to attend.
- If the power loss is general, the Duty Manager should liaise with the local utility provider.

The automatic fire detection system will last for approximately XX hours due to back-up batteries. The intruder alarms have back up batteries for XX hours.
If the power failure is going to last more than 30 minutes or it is not possible to determine how long, the museum should be closed, and the following rules should be adhered to:

- Make sure no one is trapped in the passenger lift
- Turn off any electrical appliances to prevent risk of fire and reduce likelihood of a power surge tripping the fuses when the power is restored
- Decide whether staff should remain at their work positions
- Telephone the Director/Senior Responsible Person and advise them of the situation if power failure exceeds 30 minutes. Inform pre-arranged contact list if the failure is likely to last an indefinite time
- No lifts are to be used
- No AV
- No hot desks, dishwasher, turn off all heaters, unnecessary lights and keep power use to a minimum

Once back on main power, reset all alarms, test all equipment such as AV and lifts.

Figure 6.2 *Example SOP*

your own 'suspicious device' by filling a rucksack with something like a couple of containers taped to some batteries. Throw in some museum plans and sew up the pockets for good measure. I like to leave the bag in the room during the training and see how long it takes someone to spot it. As well as good practice, this exercise livens up training days and can be good fun: just make sure your prop doesn't actually end up on the museum floor!

Fire evacuation is another thing that has to be rehearsed on the ground, from walking the evacuation routes to as many fire drills as you need in order to get it right. A new team will rarely get a fire drill right first time (we forget how difficult our buildings are for those who are unfamiliar with them) but that's where the most useful, unforgettable learning will come from.

Therefore, where you can make operational training hands-on, do so. Finally, don't expect teams to remember forever everything they have learned in their first week. This is particularly important for smaller museums, where the team might not get a chance to deal with too many different incidents in real life. As well as conducting regular exercises, pop quizzes during briefings and hiding items on site is a good way to ensure the operational muscles of your team are flexed and ready for the next thing that goes wrong.

Case Study 6: Service recovery at Stonehenge

This case study is a great example of something going very wrong, then going very right. It shows that conflict can be deescalated, and that with fantastic service recovery, even a bad visitor experience can be turned around and end up with a five-star review.

In 2021, James Rodliff was the Operations Manager at Stonehenge, the world-famous visitor attraction located near Salisbury and operated by English Heritage. 'Visitors arrive at our site with a variety of expectations' Rodliff explains. 'Stonehenge is iconic, an absolute bucket-list destination for domestic and international travellers. Although we aim to make the visitor journey as smooth and effortless as possible, there are challenges to operating such a large and complicated site with permeable boundaries, high visitor footfall and a great many moving parts' (Rodliff, 2022).

The monument itself is over 2.5 km away from the visitor centre, which features two car parks, a large café, a shop and indoor and outdoor interpretation areas, including a volunteer-run experience around the reconstructed Neolithic houses. The distance between locations necessitates a fleet of buses and a number of stops to ferry passengers through the World Heritage Site landscape. Other visitors prefer to walk and explore the landscape, or they may even arrive at the monument without passing through the visitor centre by coming across country.

'Those more "spur of the moment" visitors, or those who have been brought to our site by a third party as part of a fixed tour route, will often not know what to expect on arrival' says Rodliff. 'It is important to also consider that guests may be visiting the site with information not displayed in their own language (70% of Stonehenge visitors are from overseas) or those whose access needs have not been met by the type, form or content of pre-visit information presented to them.'

'Our amazing frontline staff and volunteer teams are the first line of defence in protecting our visitors' experiences with us' emphasises Rodliff. 'Still, they are a limited resource, often focused on critical tasks and on a busy day, especially with a site so permeable as Stonehenge, it is impossible to provide every possible level of information a visitor may require to prevent any disappointment later in their journey. We cannot always prevent disappointment, but we can be ready when it occurs. Such an occasion occurred at Stonehenge in 2021 when some of our visitors had a negative experience on our site, but the service recovery displayed by staff members made a significant impact on the outcome of their day' (Rodliff, 2022).

'Although still in the early days of recovery from the pandemic it was a busy weekend day, the early afternoon rush was in full swing and the staff were busy keeping everyone safe and happy. A call came in across the radio from one of the operations staff briefly outlining a conversation she had just had with a distressed visitor. The staff member had spotted the visitor looking upset on the return to the bus from the direction of the monument and decided to stop what they were doing and find out what was wrong. It would have been easy to let the moment slip past. There were still additional COVID-19 sanitation regimes, our staffing had not returned to normal levels, it was a busy afternoon and no doubt they would have been concerned about the potential reaction of approaching a disgruntled guest. They decided to make the approach and to politely and empathetically enquire if the visitor was okay.'

'By actively listening to the visitor the staff member had identified that the "final straw" had come from an incident where a COVID-19 "one-way" system was being too stringently (and far too firmly) enforced by a contracted steward who was less familiar with all of our processes. This would have meant the visitor was unable to reach the monument without a long walk, something she was unable to manage. The visitor was understandably very cross by the interaction and at our team collectively. Our experienced staff member knew not to take any personal offence by the situation but rather displayed personal concern and empathy. Furthermore, she immediately attempted to resolve the situation by offering additional assistance to revisit the stones together and assist with an easier access route. In the moment the visitor was too emotional and too tired to take the offer up or perhaps to even process it fully and decided to take the bus to the visitor centre and to leave.'

The steps undertaken by the Stonehenge staff member up until this point were absolutely key in starting the process of service recovery. They knew they had made a positive impact but also realised there was more that could be done. As Rodliff explains, 'this is when they took the opportunity to call the supervisor to see if there could be someone to meet them at the end of the bus ride when more time had passed, to offer additional solutions and to help resolve the issue that had resulted in this situation. Our supervisor immediately made it a priority and was present, informed and ready to help if possible.'

'They first took the visitor and companion to the café (the catering manager had overheard what was happening and had already started making them a cup of tea). The supervisor offered to sit with them and chat, not directly about the incident at first, but rather to build a rapport and be better placed to have a practical discussion away from the emotion of the incident. My supervisor knew they were not trying to win an argument, despite the contractor not being a member of their own staff, they knew this was irrelevant to the visitor and did not take this feedback personally. They did recognise that an apology costs nothing and furthermore thanked the visitor for being prepared to challenge how we do things and improve our service. After their discussion, a good cup of tea and a short but very personal tour of the exhibition with one of our volunteers, the visitors decided to leave the site as they were not able to make it back to the monument that day.'

After any incident, even one that had been turned around as successfully as this, Rodliff knew it would be important to reflect and learn lessons from what had occurred.

'Back in the office we discussed the incident at length as a team and reflected on how it went and if there were any other opportunities to improve our service' he explains. 'As a bystander to the incident, I was hugely encouraged by the actions taken by the whole team who had been part of the process of service recovery. The actions of all these individuals turned around a situation that could have resulted in a terrible experience going unchallenged, or even led to repeats of the same issue. The foresight by the first staff member to make the original approach was absolutely key and had they not had the confidence or skills to do so it would have been a significantly poorer outcome for all.'

In fact, far from having a poor outcome, the visitor in question left a five-star review for the Stonehenge team on Trip Advisor. After describing the conflict incident with the contracted security officer, the visitor writes:

> As we were looking at one of the buildings a lovely lady called Erin from English Heritage came over to find us and was so apologetic about our experience even though it was very obviously not English Heritage who was at fault. She could honestly not have been kinder or more supportive and it went a long way to making us feel better that she would go out of her way to locate us among the visitors. She offered us a complimentary visit to the café and we were very touched by this but had no real intention of taking advantage as we appreciate that English Heritage is a charity organisation and this year has suffered financially as so many have. However, when we got to the main till in the café where we had collected some drinks and some sandwiches for my son it was evident that Erin had already spoken to the people there and they asked if we were the family who had the unpleasant experience with the security guard. We confirmed that we were and they were adamant that we were not to pay a penny. They even insisted on putting some delicious rock cakes in a bag for us to take away. I really want to say a huge thank you to Erin and her team. You handled the situation so beautifully and we felt so cared for. We were very nervous taking mam for her very first outing post COVID and after the experience with the security guard we felt emotional and fragile. You absolutely turned the situation around and I feel very confident in saying that Stonehenge is a place that is accessible and welcoming to ALL.
> (Trip Advisor, 2021a).

This example demonstrates that a failure somewhere within the visit doesn't have to lead to a bad overall experience. Through great teamwork and fantastic service recovery, the Stonehenge team were able to make a real difference to this family's visit and turn a conflict into a visitor experience win.

CHAPTER 7

Performance Management

> It's important that the customer is having fun, without a doubt. But it's really important that the staff have fun too, because that impacts the customer experience.
>
> (Susan Morrison, Scotch Whisky Experience)

Whilst people may be drawn to visit a museum by the exhibitions and collections, we know that the single biggest factor in delivering an exceptional experience and driving repeat visitation is the performance and behaviour of frontline teams. To quote the much-used maxim of Bernard Donoghue, CEO of the Association of Leading Visitor Attractions, it's about 'staff, not stuff' (Donoghue, 2019).

It follows, therefore, that the most important part of managing the visitor experience is managing people and performance.

Performance management is sometimes understood as an HR process that often deals with the negative aspects of managing people; disciplinary procedures and managing people 'out'. However, like most topics I'm exploring in this book, performance management is much broader than this. It covers the managing of positive performance as well as negative, and takes in motivating teams (especially important during the quiet months of a museum operation) as well as ensuring that we as managers are developing the skills we need to support others.

Performance management should not be seen in isolation, but in the wider context of museum life. There is a clear connection between organisational culture and how staff are performance-managed. An organisation that has to deal with lots of negative performance challenges will very often find the root of the issue in the wider culture and, likewise, an organisation that generally treats its employees well will find itself with fewer disciplinary issues to contend with.

It's also important to see performance management as one part of the whole employee journey. In this book, we cover recruitment and induction in Part 1, performance management here in Part 2 and continuing professional development in Part 3. But it's really important to remember that these activities all fit together into the life cycle of one employee, and that one section can and does impact on another (Figure 7.1).

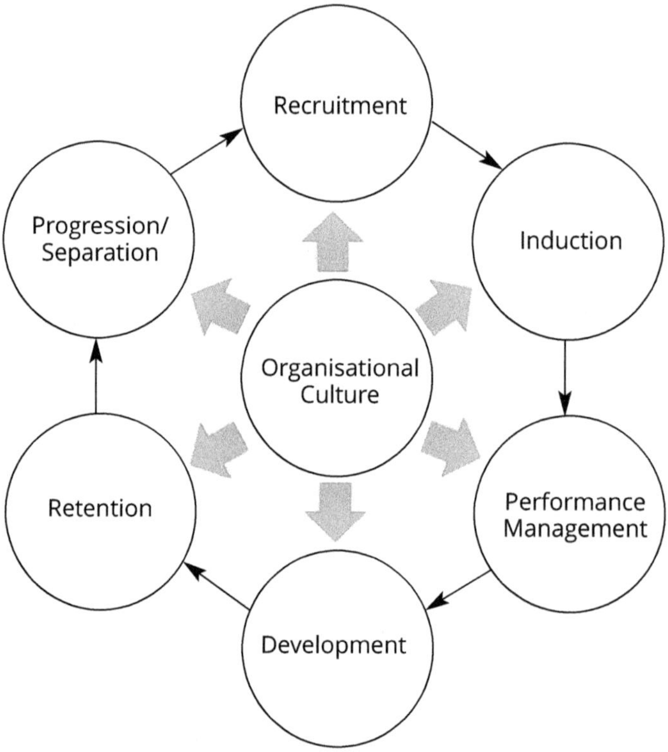

Figure 7.1 *The employee life cycle*

Performance managing diverse teams

Visitor Experience Managers can often be called on to manage large, diverse teams. People in your team might be undertaking a range of functions (as we've already discussed, Visitor Experience can mean different things in different organisations), can be on a number of different contracts, be in different stages of life and come from a variety of backgrounds.

For this reason, the first step in effective performance management, and management in general, is taking the time to get to know your people really well. The relationship between a member of staff and their line manager is one of the most important factors in job satisfaction, so it's worth putting in the effort to make sure the relationship is a good one. If you're taking on management of somebody for the first time, schedule regular one-to-ones and find out:

- What skills and experience are they bringing to the role?
- What training or information do they need to successfully do the job?
- Do they understand how what they do contributes to the museum's overall vision?
- What are their short- and long-term career goals?
- How do they best like to communicate with their manager and colleagues?
- What frustrates them about the role?
- What are they really passionate about (work-related or not)?
- What can you do to best support them?

If you find all this out at the start of the relationship, not only will you get to know each other better, you will be better prepared for any issues that arise.

If you manage many different functions within your team, you might not have direct experience of the jobs some people do. That's okay; nobody can be an expert in everything. But it's important that you make an effort to get your head around the practicalities, joys and frustrations of their role, so take the time to shadow them and see the organisation from their vantage point.

Working on the frontline at a museum is a job that can be done by people at different stages in their life, which is a huge positive. Having a large spectrum of ages in your team means you have a diversity of experience and skills you might not get in other teams. However, it can also come with challenges.

In her article 'Multiple Generations: perceptions and problems', inter-generational expert Henry Rose Lee discusses the characteristics of different generations in the workplace. Although these are obviously a generalisation, they will be familiar to many, for example the preference of the Silent Generation (born between 1925 and 1945) for formal methods of communication and the acceptance of authority, or the preference to direct their own learning and engagement shared by Generation Z (born 1997 to 2009) (Lee, 2022).

Despite different preferred workplace styles, Lee says the answer is not to treat all generations differently. Instead, she shares three key pieces of advice for managing workplaces that include multiple generations.

1 *Find the areas where these differences will matter.*
As I mentioned above, having different skills and experiences within a museum team is a great asset. It increases the team's ability to problem-solve and communicate with and welcome a wide range of visitors. So,

rather than focusing on all the differences between generations, have a think about the few areas where these differences may actually matter. For example, in giving feedback to managers, the Silent Generation may favour meetings and informal communication, whereas Millennials and Generation Z may welcome the opportunities to submit feedback in ways that suit them, whether that means online or anonymously.

2 *Find areas where differences will complement each other*
Finding areas where different skills and experiences will add value is a good way of making it clear that everyone is a respected member of the team. 'Share out tasks and learn from each other's style and ideas' says Lee. 'Some organisations call this "a dream team", where younger and older bond over a shared goal (make the deal, save the money, deliver the project, etc.). They both also recognise key yet differing attitudes and skills in each other.' For example, a common issue I have dealt with personally is managing team members much older than myself; sometimes people who have been at the organisation for decades! I've had friends from other sectors ask me about this, because I get a sense that elsewhere it isn't as common, but I've always found it to be a rewarding relationship. By showing respect for someone's length of service, you can learn whilst still providing leadership. I think the key is to be genuinely interested and open to learning new things. As someone who loves history, I always want to know the context and background to why things are done a certain way. So, if I can combine fresh new ideas with knowledge and experience, that really is a dream team!

3 *Use mentoring to build bonds, share skills and nurture talent*
Mentoring is something that happens in many organisations, with senior, often older employees helping to build on the potential of more junior staff members. But Lee also advises utilising 'reverse mentoring' 'This is where younger staff mentor older, more experienced staff. I encourage many boards of directors and senior leadership teams to choose a mentor from their youngest employees. These young mentors explain the attitudes and habits of younger workers and consumers. They share the merits of any new tech or digital apps, innovations or processes that are usually being accessed by people who are below the age of 25. It's a perfect pairing. Younger workers teach older ones about all the things they don't know about.'

I recently came across an interesting twist on this idea when I was interviewing Susan Morrison, CEO of the Scotch Whisky Experience, for the case study at the end of this chapter. One of her more recent innovations is the setting up of a 'Shadow Management Team'. As Morrison explains, 'We're going to give them some of the real-life problems and issues that we're discussing in the management team and just see whether they come up with solutions and what they come up with' (Morrison, 2022). It will be fascinating to see whether a multi-generational approach (entry-level employees in the organisation are generally younger) to problem solving makes a positive impact on business decisions at the highest level.

These tips really speak to the key feature of successfully managing diverse teams: focus on the advantages of managing a range of skills and experiences and use them to create a harmonious team and a fantastically adaptive visitor experience.

Motivation

Team motivation is a critical skill for any Visitor Experience Manager, which is why it's such a common question in interviews! The truth is that working on the frontline can often be hard: in busy periods it's full on, overwhelming and physically demanding and in quiet times the day can go slower and lethargy can set in. Longer term, staff working on the frontline can become restless without new goals to aim for. All of these circumstances require different approaches to motivation.

During busy periods, teams can lose motivation if they feel they aren't being supported, or if the operational set-up is lacking in some way. At the Natural History Museum, I held Peak Period Briefing and Peak Period Review meetings, to ensure that all feedback was captured and that teams could see the steps we were making to ensure they had everything they need for the busy period, whether that meant increased staffing or more crowd control barriers. It's also important for back-of house colleagues to be present for those really busy times. Often, busy periods like school holidays coincide with times when many back-of-house staff take leave, which can increase feelings of being unseen and under-appreciated among front-of-house teams. For those still on site, and particularly for senior managers, it's important (and extremely valuable) to spend time on the floor with your team experiencing the highs and lows of peak-period operations.

To increase that feeling of being valued, peak periods are a good time to run a peer-to-peer recognition scheme, for example when staff nominate their colleagues for good work on the floor. This can be themed to the museum values for that extra bit of organisational connectivity, but even if it isn't, just reading a nice comment from a colleague that recognises some hard work you did really makes the difference to a busy day. I know, because I still have all of mine from when I worked front of house many years ago! I implemented something similar when I was at Kew Palace, and it was really lovely giving them out and watching the Hosts read compliments from their colleagues (see Figure 7.2).

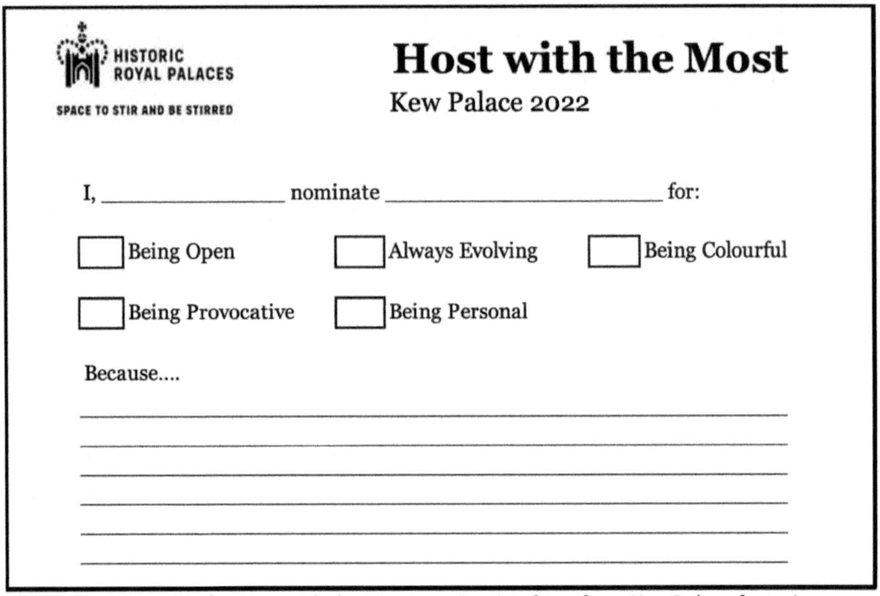

HISTORIC ROYAL PALACES

SPACE TO STIR AND BE STIRRED

Host with the Most

Kew Palace 2022

I, ______________ nominate ______________________ for:

☐ Being Open ☐ Always Evolving ☐ Being Colourful

☐ Being Provocative ☐ Being Personal

Because....

Figure 7.2 *Example of a 'Host with the Most' nomination form from Kew Palace featuring Historic Royal Palace's customer service standard*

In contrast, during quiet periods, teams have the time and energy to be challenged and driven forward in their development, so it's the perfect time to introduce new projects. The case study at the end of this chapter will show how the Scotch Whisky Experience utilises those quiet periods to drive staff engagement.

For longer-term motivation, so much depends on that individual relationship I mentioned earlier in the chapter. Only by really understanding someone's goals and interests can you tailor the development that is going to keep them high-performing and happy in their role; even if that means they will move on eventually.

Frameworks and processes

At the heart of good organisational performance management is consistency. Although different individuals might have distinctive management styles, it's really important that the same processes are followed and standards are applied consistently across an organisation. Otherwise, employees will take note of disparity of treatment, which just increases ill-feeling and discord.

The key to consistency is a good performance management framework, which means standardised paperwork for recruitment, training, performance reviews and of course, any disciplinary procedures. In larger museums, this will be supported by an HR department; however, I am aware that many organisations either contract out HR, or don't have staff specifically working on HR. My advice in this case would be to seek expert advice. If you are from a small, volunteer-led museum, for example, consider recruiting a trustee with HR expertise who can advise you.

In the UK, members of the Association of Independent Museums can access free HR advice and support through HR Dept at www.hrdept.co.uk/aim-museum. This support includes a free 15-minute consultation for urgent HR queries and free contract and handbook review. There are also a number of downloadable templates, for everything from new starter forms to exit interviews.

Performance management skills

Despite the vital importance of performance management skills, many new managers in museums come into their roles with little or no experience of people management. This is partly because we often recruit internally, promoting high performers from the frontline team. This on its own is fantastic development, but what is not fantastic is expecting new managers to look after and direct large teams without the right support and training.

Often, it's hard for people working on the frontline to gain experience at management before they are promoted. Just because you are great with visitors doesn't necessarily mean you'll be a great people manager, so if you have staff on the frontline who want to develop, try to give them a taste of the management experience so they can find out whether or not it's for them. Create those opportunities by creating half-way positions that have more supervisory responsibilities, or inviting staff to help look after volunteers.

If your museum isn't big enough to support its own performance management training course for new managers, there are many good external options out there. Many of them are pricey, but consider the lost hours, days and in the worst-case scenario, legal costs that arise from poor performance management. It's much more cost-effective to spend a bit of money on ensuring new managers are well prepared for the important task at hand.

Based on my experience, here are some (though by no means all) of the skills and qualities that make a really good people manager. These skills won't just help you keep everything plain sailing, they can also help you turn a bad situation around:

- Empathy: including the ability to understand what might be at the root of poor performance.
- Listening skills: as a manager, you should be in listening mode more often than you're in talking mode.
- Consistency: including not playing favourites, and applying standards and rules fairly. This also means embodying the values you want others to display!
- Flexibility: including the understanding that people communicate and learn in different ways.
- Persistence: sometimes performance management means checking in regularly, keeping detailed notes, reviewing, and checking in again. It can take time.
- Transparency: particularly in making any disciplinary procedure as clear and open as possible and ensuring it is by the book, including involving unions or other staff representatives.
- Advocacy: managing upwards is an important part of managing front-facing teams. It's important to represent and advocate for them when the museum management is making decisions that impact them, and ensure they are remembered and rewarded for the great work they do.
- Empowering: you should be actively working for the development of your staff, even if their goal is to take your job! Don't keep people in their place; champion them.

We'll look at ongoing engagement and development in the next part of this book.

Case Study 7: A values-based approach to motivation at the Scotch Whisky Experience

Susan Morrison, CEO of the Scotch Whisky Experience, runs a visitor attraction owned by the Scotch whisky industry in the centre of Edinburgh. During the high season, Edinburgh is extremely busy with tourists, but in January, February, November and early December, the attraction is a lot quieter, and there is more need to motivate the team and keep them engaged (Morrison, 2022).

'What we've tried to do is hang everything around our values' Morrison explains. 'We are a business that constantly refers back and talks about our values with the team.'

The values of the Scotch Whisky Experience are:

- authenticity – a natural character
- people – a warmth of spirit
- passion – a powerful blend of enthusiasm and devotion
- learning – a thirst for knowledge
- excellence – a raising of the bar
- fun – a double measure!

Authenticity

'We're very open with the staff' explains Morrison. 'So, we present strategy to them at the beginning of the year, which is obviously the quieter season. We make sure all the staff, from housekeeping to bookings, facilities to operations, get a chance to attend these sessions, just to get everyone on the same page.' Although many organisations share this sort of information with staff, many organisations do this at the start of the financial year – which obviously coincides with the school holidays. Often, the museum calendar is dictated by Finance and HR processes. The Scotch Whisky Experience shows how much more valuable these sessions can be if they are done at a time when frontline teams have the bandwidth to properly engage with the material.

People

The Scotch Whisky Experience also uses quieter times to drive forward development of its people.

'We let the staff do a lot of projects during the low season' Morrison says. 'One of the team is very interested in marketing and he came up with a campaign for locals; the "Under your nose" campaign; a brilliant idea for us that we ran with. He helped the marketing team roll out this campaign, which we wouldn't have had, had the team not been encouraged to undertake low season projects.' Another example shows that this development doesn't necessarily need to remove staff from the floor, rather, the team take advantage of the decreased visitor numbers by multitasking. 'We will ask some of the team to write blogs to give marketing additional content. It's something you can do at the box office if there are no visitors, so there are some projects that can be done whilst they're actually in position on the floor.' These projects are voluntary, but if the team want to develop their talents in particular areas, they are welcome to use the down time afforded by the low season to do so.

Performance review timetables have also been adjusted to take the seasons into account. 'For the frontline departments that are very busy in the higher season, we try to get our reviews done in the quieter periods, which is just sensible, but it is also motivating because it gives individuals time to think about what they want to get out of their review. It's a much more relaxed atmosphere for the reviewer and the reviewee at this time of year and it makes the review far more productive and beneficial for all. They'll even get more of a chance to work on objectives or undertake a bit of training that's come out of the review.'

Passion

The formal training programme for frontline staff at the Scotch Whisky Experience provides them with everything they need to know, but what excites Morrison is seeing that spark igniting into a flame as staff head off in their own time to learn more about the industry. Frequently, staff take holidays in order to visit distilleries on their own bringing back more knowledge and more enthusiasm to the team. Managers do what they can to encourage this, as Morrison explains: 'we'll facilitate visits by picking up the phone and letting distilleries know that a member of the team is visiting, so they get well looked after, but it's their own time and money, which is amazing.'

Learning

In terms of learning, Morrison says contacts within the whisky industry are an excellent and inspiring resource which can be called upon during quiet periods. 'Our industry shareholders and stakeholders afford us access to amazing expertise. We will run sessions for the team with master blenders and master distillers, the celebrities of the industry, in the quieter period. It's motivating to have these whisky celebs come in and talk – not only is their expertise invaluable but their passion is infectious.'

Excellence

During the low season, the management team will also send staff out to undertake benchmarking exercises at other Edinburgh attractions, not just to look for good ideas that can be used in the business but also to improve the team's local knowledge to better assist visitors. There is also time for the staff forum to go through mystery shopper reports. 'They make sure they communicate all the good stuff to ensure we're celebrating the wins, as well as dealing with any actions.'

Fun

'Our last value is fun, and that's important', Morrison explains. 'It's important that the customer is having fun, without a doubt. But it's really important that the staff have fun too, because that impacts the customer experience. So, amongst other things we have an absolutely rigid programme of pre-season and post-season parties. The pre-season party takes the form of team games and challenges and serves as a great way for all the staff in all departments to get to know each other in advance of the high season. The post-season party is a glitzy, glamorous affair, and it's more of a thank you. We run an award ceremony followed by a three-course meal served in our Amber restaurant. The leadership team run the entire event. We cook (we have a chef on the leadership team), serve and clear up as well as hosting the award ceremony. It never fails to amaze me how motivating it is for the team to see us cook, serve dinner, and then wash up the dishes whilst they're enjoying themselves in the bar.'

The Scotch Whisky Experience is such a great example of how taking the lead from your organisational values can help drive performance management. Rather than seeing the low season as a time they have to get through, Morrison and her team use it as an opportunity to drive development and engagement in a positive way.

Perhaps the biggest lesson to come out of this case study is the way Morrison has reshaped the business year to fit with high and low season, moving financial updates and performance reviews away from the times that traditionally fit with Finance and HR processes in favour of times that work better for delivery teams.

In fact, it was having access to a different sector that inspired that change, as Morrison explains:

'What really hammered it home for me was being out and about with the distillers. Traditionally distilleries have a silent season when there's less water available (distilleries need a lot of water), so this is usually July. That means the distillery is not operating at this time and general maintenance is undertaken, but that's also when a lot of visitors want to visit. I used to think that was crazy; absolutely crazy from the visitor experience side. A lot of them have since managed to change this, but that's what first made me think, why on earth would we be doing some of our essential processes at a time that's not right for the business? Seeing this happen in another industry made me realise we do a bit of the same in our own business; we do these things at really bad times because it fits with our business processes.'

So have a look at your traditional business calendar. By placing the delivery teams and the visitors front and centre, you could turn your quiet period into an opportunity for development and engagement, and ultimately positive performance management.

CHAPTER 8

Emotion and the Visitor Experience

> The personal preferences, unique background, and prior knowledge of each participant affected how they reacted to what they saw.
>
> (McLellan and Douglas, 2004, 58)

Museums and cultural organisations exist not just to preserve the past, but to have an impact on the future through inspiring change in their visitors. Exactly how to best define and demonstrate this impact has been a source of some debate in the museum community, but one concept that has emerged as central to impact is that of 'emotion'.

In early museum studies, the idea of engaging with emotion was seen as a distraction from the fact-based, authoritative voice museums should have. Museums were considered to be objective and expert arbiters of facts, with no room to engage with a concept as vague and subjective as emotion (Smith and Campbell, 2015). However, more recent research into audience impact has highlighted the benefits of engaging with emotion, especially when dealing with some of the stories left out by the traditional museum approaches of the past. Developing programmes or exhibitions which deliberately deal with emotional content can help visitors experience greater impact, make deeper connections and ultimately, even create positive change.

There is little doubt that engaging in emotion work in museums has real benefits. However, when deliberately targeting visitor emotion, it is vitally important that we also consider possible negative effects on the visitor, and in turn, the impact this can have on our frontline teams.

The impact on Visitor Experience staff

As we have seen above, there are good reasons to design emotion into museum experiences. Used wisely, programming that targets audience emotion can have a greater impact on our visitors, enable them to make deeper connections and even inspire positive behaviour change. But in order to say we have used it wisely we have to consider the impact emotional programming has on the jobs of frontline staff.

We've probably all had museum and heritage experiences that have affected us deeply. Some examples would clearly be challenging and deeply troubling to come face to face with, like a charred child's lunchbox at the Hiroshima Memorial Peace Museum, or nooses displayed at Kingston Lacy representing men hanged for homosexuality. For me, I think about the time I visited Dachau, or the Holocaust exhibition at the Imperial War Museum, as experiences which have felt important but hard; where you might even have to take a break before heading back into the horror. We know how critical it is that we have these lessons taught to us, we know how important it is to remember; but it's a hard journey none the less.

These extreme feelings normally don't last forever; we might shake them off as soon as we step outside the museum, or with the experiences that have touched us deeply, we might be affected for a few days, resolving to take action to help right whatever wrong we have been made aware of.

Frontline staff in these museums or exhibitions don't have the luxury of shaking off such experiences. They live in them constantly, face to face with emotional triggers and unpredictable visitor reactions every day. This is not to say the role isn't a valuable one – staffing emotionally impactful exhibitions or programmes can be a rich learning experience, and if your organisation is using emotional programming to advocate change, working front of house means that you have a front-row seat to witness that change. It can be a real honour. But too often, the experience of frontline staff is an afterthought for design teams who may have already moved on to the next project before the first visitor has even entered the exhibition. In projects like these, I often see evidence that audience support has been well thought out; trigger warnings as part of the interpretation or signposting for support services. But the main way we can look after audiences is by ensuring the staff on the ground are able and willing to help. And this means looking after the staff on the ground themselves.

There's another aspect to this too. Sometimes our stories can draw the wrong kind of attention. 'Culture wars' are all too prevalent in our media these days, with museum and heritage organisations often being accused of 'wokery' for exploring previously untold aspects of history. Whilst staff might understandably be worried about visitor reactions, there is real power to our interactions in these spaces. People are far more likely to consider something in a new way after a conversation in a place where relevant history happened than after a spat on Twitter. By positively engaging in these topics, we can become advocates for a more nuanced conversation; cultural peacekeepers in an age of manufactured conflict. But to do so, we have to get training and support for our front-facing teams absolutely right.

Supporting Visitor Experience staff

When working in emotionally impactful spaces, frontline staff are grappling with three interlinked responsibilities: their responsibility to telling the story and delivering the content, which is, after all, the goal of the exhibition or project; their responsibility to look after visitors; and their responsibility to look after themselves. So, I find that when thinking about supporting these teams, it helps to think in the same way, as illustrated in Figure 8.1.

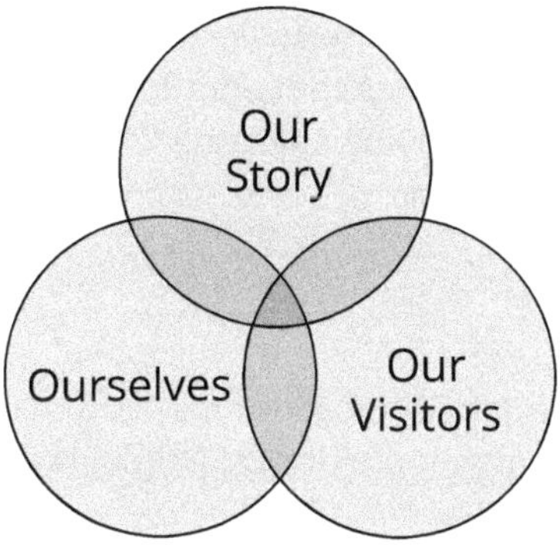

Figure 8.1 *Model for supporting teams with emotionally challenging content*

Our story

When dealing with stories that can be challenging or provocative, it's important to make sure your teams are confident with the facts. Ensure there is plenty of time before the exhibition opens or the programme begins for Visitor Experience staff to become familiar with the content, so that they can describe and explain it in their own way, rather than quote curatorial texts or books. Make sure they understand the relevance of the topic to your museum: why are we telling this story? Within some topics, there might be terminology that is used in historical sources on display, but is no longer appropriate. Make sure there is time to get all this straight, and whilst the team are learning (which could be throughout the lifetime of the exhibition or project), they are doing so in a supportive, non-judgemental atmosphere.

When delivering information to your team, ensure that all the delivery isn't coming from one place. As a management team, you may not have the right personnel to speak with authority on some of the more challenging topics, so use external experts where necessary. The project team should have consulted external experts on the development of the exhibition or project; see if some of this resource can be utilised to support your team where necessary, for example by commissioning an external expert to help you lead some induction training for your team. Ideally, get these requests captured right at the beginning, so it becomes a regular part of scoping out a project and not an ad hoc ask.

Finally, remember that facts are important, but context is even more so. There are a million different ways to tell one story, so sense-check the content your team are delivering to make sure it's framed within the correct context. Are there narratives that are left out or missing? What questions might visitors ask next? What is the contemporary relevance – how does the content relate to what is happening now? Thinking all this through at the start will lead to less awkward silences on the gallery floor, and a more confident team on the ground. These are things that should have been considered by the project team/curator, so ask them to help get this context across to your team, and ultimately, to your visitors.

Our visitors

The most important thing to think about here is that every visitor will have a different reaction to what you are doing. Think about this example from the Pitt Rivers Museum.

In 2002/3, the *Objects Talk* exhibition at the Pitt Rivers Museum displayed a variety of objects from the collection chosen and interpreted by community groups, including young asylum seekers (McLellan and Douglas, 2004). During the interpretation project, staff members Andrew McLellan and Oliver Douglas found that every member of their community group related to the individual objects differently: 'The personal preferences, unique background, and prior knowledge of each participant affected how they reacted to what they saw' (McLellan and Douglas, 2004, 58). The prior experiences of the group were all so different that McLellan and Douglas could never have predicted how they would react to the objects. In the same way, we can never predict how visitors will react to the content we choose to put out into the world. Although full of exciting possibilities, this also throws up the challenge of preparing frontline staff to deal with a myriad of possible visitor reactions and emotions.

Therefore, the first step in planning to deal with visitors is to understand and accept different responses, and to make sure Visitor Experience staff know that this is anticipated and accepted too. Then, for the tiny, tiny minority of situations where the visitor will have such an extreme reaction to emotional content that it actually causes an operational issue, the staff need to be clear about how this will be dealt with on the day. Most of the conversations staff have with visitors will be positive and easily managed. But they should still know what to do now if they are faced with a visitor who is in crisis, or who has a really negative reaction.

These responses can range from the sort of techniques taught in mental health first aid courses, to signposting visitors to support, to having quiet spaces where visitors can sit and gather their thoughts. There's also the possibility that visitors will react to content (however illogically) in ways that are abusive or aggressive, especially if the content falls into the arena of the so-called 'culture wars'. Procedures to deal with this can include having a Duty Management team trained in conflict resolution or radio code words to get an immediate security response. It's up to you to fit the how and what to the situation; what your team need to know is that you have thought through the 'what happens if?'

Ourselves

Finally, it's important to have wellbeing support in place for front-of-house teams. This should be true of any museum, but especially true for those putting on challenging or provocative content.

During the COVID-19 pandemic, there was an explosion in wellbeing activity for staff, so it's not hard to find inspiration if this is something your museum is lacking. Employee Assistance Programmes, where staff can access free, anonymous counselling services, are really valuable, and sometimes you can refer on behalf of someone else if you are concerned. If you promote these services in your museum, make sure the contact details and information are somewhere easily accessible, but also private, such as posters in bathrooms.

As well as the more formal services, I've been aware of organisations providing mindfulness sessions, yoga, financial planning, nutrition talks, exercise classes and a whole host of other activities to promote wellbeing in teams. Fit the resources you have to the needs of your team as best as you can, but remember, yoga is no substitute for knowing your team, good communication and managers who care. So, before throwing a lot of activities at your team to see what sticks, have a really good think about what they actually need, and what they might need on top of that to support the emotionally impactful programming you might be planning next. If you're not sure what this might be, talk to the team and see what they want and need to secure their emotional wellbeing at work.

Case Study 8: Kew Palace and George III

I'm going to use an example from my own experience for this case study, and it's not because I think we got everything right from the start, but because we had a good learning curve to work with. A lot of the interventions I'm going to discuss here grew up organically rather than us thinking about it beforehand, and we were lucky that we had a lot of experience to draw on. Still, I hope that some of what we learnt can be useful when planning for supporting and developing front-of-house teams.

King George III is probably best known for his famous periods of mental ill-health which meant he was unable to rule for months at a time, and led to his son, Prince George, being installed as Prince Regent in 1811. During his episodes of ill-health, he often came to Kew Palace to recover. In 2021, this famous story was retold in *George III: The Mind Behind the Myth* (HRP, 2020), a new exhibition focusing on historical and contemporary attitudes to mental health. Wellbeing is an important subject; never more so following a year of lockdown, and it felt like the perfect time to re-examine this topic from a contemporary standpoint.

When it came to planning how I would prepare and support our Host team and visitors for the exhibition, there was plenty of experience to draw on. Although we hadn't previously focused on the King's mental health, it was always one of the few things that visitors knew about him, so the Hosts faced constant questions on the topic. This meant that they had to be fully briefed on the facts of the case, including using the right terminology. The Hosts had also shared a fact that really inspired the exhibition: when visitors started talking about George III and mental health, they would often start talking about mental health in general, even disclosing stories about themselves or their loved ones. This is such a brilliant example of what history can do, the impact it can have and the doors it can open. But it also meant that if we wanted to delve into the subject in detail, we had to be prepared to deal with a wide range of visitor reactions.

I used the model discussed here – Our Story, Our Visitors, Ourselves – to make sure that as we planned for the exhibition, I was taking everything we had already learned from our visitors into account.

Our story

We had a seasonal team at Kew Palace, so we were able to do a lot of off-gallery training during the induction period, with curators coming in and doing tours and talks. However, when it came to the King's mental health, we knew we had to consider more than just delivering the facts. Terminology and attitudes have changed a lot over the last 200 years, and the Hosts had to consider the impact their words had when talking about mental health; every visitor brings their own experiences to the Palace after all. So, we started teaching Hosts the story of his ill health as part of a wider session called 'Talking about Mental Health'. As well as telling the story of the King, along with the different positions historians have taken over the years on the nature of his illness, we looked at mental health in a contemporary context, myth-busting with the latest statistics and making sure everyone was aware of the correct terminology.

One of the main things we learnt from visitors was that everyone is desperate to know what was wrong with the King. Theories on this have evolved over the years from porphyria to bipolar disorder, but the truth is that we could never, and probably should never, attempt to diagnose specific conditions over a void of two centuries. More worryingly, in the past, diagnoses of George III have taken on the hue of value-laden judgements, with porphyria at times seemingly the preferred condition, as it is a physical illness with psychological symptoms, as opposed to a mental illness (HRP, 2020). Because these diagnoses can be so fraught, during the induction sessions I encouraged the Hosts to redirect visitors away from the mystery-solving aspects of what the condition was, and to think about the bigger issues raised by the historiography.

For this, it was really useful for me to be part of some of the sessions led by my colleagues in the Public Engagement team. To help inform the interpretation of the exhibition, the team worked with a group of men with lived experience of mental ill-health to talk about the issues that resonated with them. One of the conversations that really struck a chord with me was a discussion around the importance of diagnosis. Some of the men were saying that often they feel diagnosis is more important for the people around them. Obviously, it's critical that illness is diagnosed and understood correctly in order to enable effective treatment, but they also felt that other people (even friends and family members) were more comfortable when they could label them, as if they now fitted into a neat category that was easily understood. To me, that comment really chimed with visitors always wanting to diagnose King George. Enabling my Host team to also have the opportunity to talk to the community group participants helped them discuss the diagnosis issue with visitors in a sensitive way, relating it to contemporary experience and allowing a deeper conversation beyond 'so what was wrong with him?'

So, when I talk about getting the 'Our Story' part right, often it isn't just about what the story is, but how we tell it. To get this right at Kew, it was really important that we:

(a) listened to external experts, and
(b) had Visitor Experience teams involved in those exhibition development conversations right from the start.

I think these two points are critical and can be transferred to any exhibition or project that deals with emotional content.

Our visitors

When it came to preparing staff to deal with 'our visitors', we were talking about a huge variety of possible reactions. As I've already mentioned, visitors bring their own history to your experience, and reactions and emotions can be unpredictable. We had to prepare Hosts for pleasant conversations and personal crises, and everything in between.

One of the first things we did to prepare for this was have the management team all undergo Mental Health First Aid training. Through doing this, not only did we all become a lot more familiar and comfortable discussing mental health at work, but we were equipped with the knowledge to deal with someone in crisis, and could pass that on to our Hosts. Because Kew Palace is a visitor attraction at the end of the day, staff were equipped to signpost rather than counsel, but we put a Mental Health First Aid kit in the Palace as well as a regular First Aid kit, so that Hosts had somewhere they could pick up leaflets, numbers for helplines, even tissues if visitors got upset. We also covered the safeguarding of vulnerable adults in our induction training. In fact, this was all stuff we had had in place since 2018. In preparing for the 2021 exhibition, we went further, asking one of our partners, the suicide prevention organisation CALM (Campaign Against Living Miserably) to give all of our Hosts the same training they give their own volunteers. This was especially important in preparing the team to talk about some of the contemporary items on display in the exhibition, one of which related to suicide.

Ourselves

Finally, we needed to make sure that the Hosts were looking after themselves, and not taking the emotional heft of the exhibition home with them. One important element of this was being really open about mental wellbeing right from the start of their employment journey with us. From the initial interview, we talked about mental health being a big theme for us, and why it was important in a contemporary context. Then, by delivering our 'Talking about Mental Health' session right in their first week, and making sure they knew that all the resources we recommended to visitors were available for staff as well, we created an open and supportive environment. The reason I know this is because the first year we introduced this session was the first time some Hosts opened up as dealing with mental health issues in their pre-season health questionnaires. I don't think that these were issues that had materialised over the winter, I think that for the first time, they felt confident that they wouldn't be judged or misunderstood.

Ahead of our exhibition, we added more resource towards supporting staff with mindfulness sessions provided by an external counsellor, increased signposting of our Employee Assistance programme and other corporate wellbeing activities and arranged a session with a counsellor for our team leaders, so that they could talk through any concerns they had about managing staff who were going through a hard time with their mental health.

It's important to say that all this activity didn't go perfectly. There were times when I felt we could have done more, and others where I worried we had gone so far down the counsellor route that we were no longer effective managers: spending hours and hours sitting with individual team members and leaving the rest of the team to fend for themselves. But overall, by using the 'Our Story, our Visitors, Ourselves' model, by getting to know our team really well and by remembering that support and development has to extend beyond the induction training, I think we created an environment where the Hosts felt confident supporting visitors through a transformative visitor experience, and leave them thinking differently about mental health.

CHAPTER 9

Guided Tours

> Guests come away feeling informed and entertained having spent time in these special, secret spaces.
>
> (Oliver Burton, London Transport Museum)

One aspect of museum programming or interpretation that Visitor Experience staff are often involved in delivering personally is the guided tour.

Like many aspects of museum practice, guided tours have gone through peaks and troughs of popularity over the years. We are all familiar with the classic pitfalls of the guided tour offer: the monologuing tour guide, the over-reliance on facts and figures, and strict historic-house hosts who seem to rule their group with a rod of iron (Vagnone and Ryan, 2016). But there are far more examples where museum tour guiding is done really well: and in these instances, we find that tours can be a great way to provide a personalised, rich and dynamic experience to your visitors. In this chapter, we will look at the pros and cons of guided tours, and ways to develop a tour – and more importantly, develop tour guides – to keep your visitors engaged and coming back for more.

Pros and cons of guided tours

There are pros and cons to face-to-face tour guiding, summed up in Table 9.1, but actually all the research points to them as being a sure-fire way to increase visitor satisfaction. In fact, many studies show that not only do visitors have a more enjoyable experience if they take part in guided tours (Huang, Weiler

Table 9.1 *Pros and cons of guided tours*

Pros	Cons
Increased visitor satisfaction	Can be seen as didactic
Encourages repeat visitation	Less opportunity to explore
Sense of security for the visitor	Intellectually unchallenging

and Assaker, 2014, 354), they are also more likely to visit again (Weiler and Black, 2015, 92).

Tours can also provide a sense of security for visitors. Rather than having to decide for themselves which are the important highlights of a museum, a curated tour takes the pressure off and leaves them in the hands of experts. There's also a social aspect to this security. Group activities provide opportunities to encounter the new and unexpected – which for many is a key motivator for experiencing culture – in the safety of the collective (Schmidt, 1979, 443).

On the other side of the coin, there can be perceived disadvantages to guided tours. First is the accusation that tours are didactic: people talk at you, not with you. As a tourist on a guided tour, it can be easy to spectate rather than participate (Schmidt, 1979, 444), and slip into a lethargy of disengagement where very little learning or enjoyment can be gained from the experience. However, I would argue that this con can be mitigated with the skill of a good tour guide. We'll explore these skills, and tools for tour engagement, later.

Secondly, it can be argued that tours don't challenge visitors intellectually (Schmidt, 1979, 444), as they have to be pitched to the lowest common denominator. While the challenge of delivering one tour to a large number of people can make this a possibility, a good tour guide should be able to read the level of audience engagement to pitch information at the right educational level, and allow space for discussion and elaboration of key points where possible.

A step-by-step guide to planning a guided tour

Whilst there can be cons to the guided tour, developing and delivering tours with well-planned content and a skilled tour team can mitigate many of these issues. So, if you are planning a new tour offer for your museum and heritage site, here are some key things to think about:

1. Assess the practicalities

In heritage buildings, the shape and offer of your tour will very often be dictated or limited to a certain extent by the practicalities of the building. For example:

- What is the capacity of each space on the tour? Will this change under certain circumstances, e.g. at an event with drinks or under COVID-19 restrictions?

- Is the tour accessible to all and if not, what adjustments can be made?
- What are the risks to your visitors and staff? For example, does the tour take them over any difficult terrain or ground, or into any restricted spaces?
- What is the procedure if somebody on the tour is injured or falls ill?

All of the above should be covered in a tour risk assessment which should be shared and discussed with the guides, and available for visitors should they wish to see it.

There are other things to think about that wouldn't necessarily feature in a risk assessment but need to be considered as part of your planning, for example any sound issues. You could have a room with particularly dodgy acoustics or an AV track that needs to be switched off.

If you're planning a tour whilst the space is open to general visitors, you'll also have to plan how the tour group and visitors work around each other. Often in this case, it's useful to have a member of staff 'tail-ending' the tour. This person can help the tour group stay together and make sure general visitors don't accidentally end up joining, all the while leaving the tour guide free to concentrate on their job. Careful route planning can also mitigate this issue. When we ran tours at the Natural History Museum, we made sure the route focused on the quieter galleries and routes and avoided congested areas.

2. What is your story?

Some sites have a clear story, for example the history of a particular family or event. People working at other types of sites, for example museums with large, disparate collections, might struggle more to find a narrative that joins the tour together. But it's important that that narrative thread is found, simply because storytelling packs a stronger emotional punch.

A research study of Chinese visitors to Sovereign Hill, a heritage site in Victoria, Australia, (Huang, Weiler and Assaker, 2014) posited that to develop an effective guided tour, a balance has to be struck between cognition (what visitors think) and their affective state (how they feel). In other words, it's not enough just to teach people a new fact or a new intellectual concept. It's also not enough to just target their emotions. You need to do both. So, a good tour has to have cognitive-affective impact (Huang, Weiler and Assaker, 2014, 345). In other words, it has to make them think and it has to make them feel.

Accuracy is important. To ensure this, collaboration with colleagues across the organisation is key. For example, colleagues working in interpretation and curatorial teams can work with you to develop tour content, or ensure that if you develop it within your team, that it speaks to the key messages the organisation is trying to get across, and that facts and research shared is accurate and up to date.

Try to weave in moments of surprise. As we've discussed, taking a guided tour provides psychological security in that it takes away the stress of having to plan for oneself which elements of the museum to see and which to miss out. However, in doing so, the visitor sacrifices an element of choice or freedom they might otherwise have enjoyed (Schmidt, 1979, 447). The key to the success of this exchange is ensuring that the visitor doesn't feel they have made the wrong bargain, by giving up on the opportunity for adventure or the unexpected in favour of the predictability of a guided tour. By adding these elements back in, and by injecting some unexpected aspect within the experience, we leave visitors feeling that they have made the right choice.

For example, at Kew Palace, my favourite thing to do on a tour was tell visitors about the wing of the building where King George III was kept when he was mentally ill. I gesture at a door through which he would have been taken, then open the door to reveal a brick wall. The Victorians demolished that section of the building so that all that remains is the external wall, and I liked to refer to it as a symbol of the Victorian attitude to mental health. Visitors love the metaphor, but they love getting to see behind a closed door even more!

Once you've got your story sorted, put it together with the work you've done on the logistics. In the past, I've found it helpful to give delivery staff a guide with all the stages of the tour worked out along with what health and safety measures need to be considered at that stage, bullet points of the content they should hit and a rough guide to how much time should be spent in each area. Table 9.2 opposite is an example of the sort of guide we might create for part of a tour at Kew Palace.

3. Who are your audience?

Depending on whether your tour is aimed at school groups, international visitors, families or adults, its content will need to be reshaped in very different ways. For example, there is an 18th-century wet larder at the Royal Kitchens at Kew with meat hooks in the ceiling. I used to refer to it as 'the Fifty Shades of Grey' room, but only on the adult evening tours once visitors had had a glass of wine!

However, considering the audience doesn't just mean pitching the content at the right level. The authors of the Sovereign Hill research study found that tours were more effective when content could be linked to the background of the tour group, who in this case were Chinese (Huang, Weiler and Assaker, 2014, 355). Putting this into practice more generally, the example highlights

Table 9.2 *Example of a tour framework guide*

Stage	Actions	Safety Information	Tour Content
Outside	Introduction and overview. Ensure nobody is carrying food and drink. Any large bags?	Follow any instructions from the Host if the fire alarm goes off.	Samuel Fortrey built Kew Palace in 1631. Royal family in residence at the White House. Took lease for Kew Palace in 1728. Relationship between George II and Frederick, Prince of Wales. Role of Kew Palace throughout life of George III: Schoolhouse, holiday home, place of recuperation and treatment.
King's Antechamber	Ensure all group can see object case. Introduce bust of King George III.	N/A	Madame Tussaud bust of George III: to celebrate Golden Jubilee in 1810. Last time he was seen in public.
King's Library	Stand by the fireplace so that the group can easily see both walls, the object case and the fresco above the fireplace.	Ensure group keep their distance from the barrier in front of the paintings.	George III had a collection of 65,000 books and was taught architecture and geometry here at Kew. Story of his marriage to Charlotte. Uncovered fresco on wall.

the importance of employing tour guides who can relate to specific audiences. At a very basic level, this means recruiting for skills such as relevant languages, but it's also worth thinking about selecting tour guides who can relate to the intended audience at a deeper level. For example, when we talk about 'hard-to-reach audiences' in museums (a misnomer, as it's usually the museum that is hard to reach for some audiences rather than the other way around) it's easy to understand why some groups struggle to feel welcome in museums when they don't see their experiences and backgrounds reflected not just in the content, but in the staff themselves.

4. Invest in training

In an earlier chapter, we discussed that the best connection between the museum and your audience will always be through people. This means that the most important element of any tour is not the content, the location or the subject; it's the tour guide.

The role of the tour guide

A skilled tour guide has to perform several roles at once. They must act as an interpreter for the museum, illuminating certain aspects for the visitor whilst protecting them from a barrage of overwhelming information. They must tell the story of their museum or heritage site whilst ensuring that balance of cognitive-affective impact is being delivered. They need to read their audiences, picking up on areas of interest, common ground and attention spans. Then, like a great dinner party host, they have to ensure engagement flows freely, not just between the museum and the visitor, or even the guide and the visitor, but between the visitors themselves. And they have to do all this whilst considering and managing the operational aspects of the tour, like timings, group size, making sure the group doesn't get in the way of other visitors, and even managing challenging visitor behaviour.

A guide therefore has to fulfil an intellectual, an emotional, a social and a practical role – and all at the same time. And, as impossible as this may sound, the first step to achieving this is understanding that no one role is more important than the other. Without the basic knowledge to deliver the history of the site, a tour falls apart, but it also falls apart if a guide fails to engage the emotions of the audience, or makes a section of the tour too long or too short. All these roles must be working in harmony to deliver a successful tour. Given the challenge this presents, it should come as no surprise that good training is absolutely essential for tour guides.

Tour guide training and development

Tour guide training is a practice that is becoming increasingly formalised and recognised in the tourism industry, especially as visitors become more discerning about the experiences they take part in and their expectations rise accordingly (Weiler and Black, 2015, 116). In some museums, however, tour training is still delivered in more of an ad-hoc way, with guides learning on the job with colleagues. Practical training like this can be very effective, and I would certainly argue that any tour training programme must include practical elements. However, I would also advocate training that is less ad-hoc and more planned. As I have outlined above, tour guiding is not an easy job, and it's important that organisations respect the challenge and skill involved by investing time and resource in well thought-out training programmes.

When designing a tour training programme, think about the roles I mentioned above – intellectual, emotional, social and practical – and make sure you are creating training interventions that target those skills and competencies.

The intellectual competencies (knowing the content you wish to impart) are probably the easiest area to provide training in, as it can be done in a number of ways, depending on different learning styles. Guides can conduct private research through books, film, podcasts, etc. or learn from curators or other experts within the museum. As a manager, I would always encourage guides to delve deeper into their personal areas of interest, because speaking about something they are really excited about lends an authentic passion to their delivery. However, I would also caution that not every visitor is likely to share this interest. In other words, just because you are violently passionate about the architectural details of a particular room doesn't mean everyone else will be.

This is where those softer skills come in; the emotional and social roles. Developing skills in these areas will help leverage the intellectual foundation a guide has built into a personalised, relevant and unique tour. To develop the emotional skills needed for tour delivery, encourage guides to find the emotional resonance and human interest in their stories. Franklin Vagnone and Deborah Ryan, authors of *Anarchist's Guide to Historic House Museums*, have written in detail on this, and encourage us to think about tour details that might have stuck in our own minds:

> We do not remember any of those dates nor, certainly, any of the numbers. Instead, we remember hearing the sound of the bells the servants heard when being summoned; the indentation in the stone steps made from years of use; the markings on wallpaper made by the family's mischievous teenagers; the corn cob pipe the nanny smokes when rocking the children to sleep. We remember the short stories, not as chapters in a novel, but as distinct moments when we felt an emotional, empathetic connection with the people who once lived there.
>
> (Vagnone and Ryan, 2016, 105)

Asking guides to take part in this remembering exercise as part of their training could be a great way to get them into the habit of finding and prioritising the emotional resonance. Storytelling training is also a good way to get into this mindset, and there are various companies, at least in the UK, who can deliver this training for cultural attractions. Vagnone and Ryan also highlight brevity when it comes to storytelling, using this famous, unattributed short story to prove that you don't need a high word count to pack a strong emotional punch: 'For sale: baby shoes, never worn' (p. 106).

When it comes to developing the skills needed for the social role of the tour guide, the first lesson to be learnt is the importance of sacrificing the ego! Tours are not an opportunity to show off how much we know; they are an opportunity to inspire our visitors and perhaps even change their way of thinking. For this to happen, visitors need to feel welcome, comfortable and listened to. So, forget the word 'guide' for a moment, and instead consider the word 'host'. A good host wouldn't monologue at guests, they would let them bring their own experiences and ideas to the party. They would know their guests intimately and draw on common ground to help the group to come together. As Vagnone and Ryan (p. 83) advise: 'Rather than starting with a lecture . . . presentations should begin by learning about the guests' personal interests. Be careful not to sound like a know-it-all, and try to draw out differing opinions and perspectives.' On a tour, I've found it effective to start off with a very basic, brief introduction to the topic. This helps you get a feeling for how much your visitors might know already, and whether they are keen to learn from your expertise, or have more of a conversation where they get to enjoy telling you some facts; either is perfectly valid as a visitor experience. Make sure your introduction doesn't include any assumed knowledge on the part of your guests, make sure you have a few simple ways to set the context, and go from there.

There are lots of ways to develop these social skills before actually delivering a tour. Try getting guides to deliver a practice tour for colleagues, and encourage them to use their knowledge of the people involved to build rapport and drive the direction of the content. Or, ask them to practise these skills on a one-to-one basis, getting into conversation with visitors in the museum and using some easy, open-ended questions like 'Where have you travelled from?' or 'Who is your favourite artist?' to start a conversation and get to know them better. Doing this will help them practise turning these audience insights into great, relevant content that relates both to the visitors and to your museum, whilst at the same time delivering a valuable interaction for the visitors involved.

Finally, developing the practical skills needed to manage a tour can be handled in a number of ways. Things like time management and route management become harder when a tour isn't memorised word for word, so in the more personal approach that I'm advocating for this requires those skills to become habitual. Luckily, things like punctuality and being aware of your surroundings are traits that we recruit for in Visitor Experience anyway, so they should be ready-baked into our tour guides. If there is a member of staff who struggles with time management in general, chances are they aren't going to be a good tour guide either, no matter how knowledgeable or charming they are. Remember, the practical skills are just as important as everything else here, so those basic abilities are really critical. If they aren't there, that's a performance management issue, but you can help develop them in the tour context by asking them to time-keep for other tour guides, providing signals when time is running out or they need to move on. This can help make keeping one eye on the clock habitual, and get them familiar with how long it takes to get from A to B.

There are always some site-specific practicalities that pop up on a tour: things like making sure AV in one room is switched off because the noise bleeds through, or making sure a door is closed because otherwise it forms a wind tunnel and that other door slams shut: the quirks and fancies of the often historic and always temperamental buildings that we work in. Those practicalities really do have to be learned on the job, and shadowing or buddying with established tour guides is a great way to achieve that.

However, there are also some practicalities you can think about and tool-up for beforehand. For example, it's really important to encourage tour guides to think through scenarios for dealing with challenging visitor behaviour, as this is something that can throw a tour wildly off course if left unchecked.

Strategies for dealing with challenging behaviour can range from the soft (for example, gently using humour to prod the tour back on course), to the hard (calling a manager for support and possible ejection of a visitor), and your organisation may well have policies and procedures on how much you are willing to put up with. What's important is that the tour guides are also aware of the parameters they are working within, and are confident in the support they have from you as their manager. Try working through some different examples of visitor conflict and discuss ways of dealing with it as a group. You might even want to employ role play to give them some practical experience. Even if it's just a conversation, working through a variety of examples will help new guides become familiar with ways of handling visitors and ensure that they have a consistent approach. I've included some examples of this in Table 9.3 on the next page, but of course it might be slightly different, depending on the requirements of each site.

Finally, it's important to remember that tour guide training should not be something that happens once at the beginning of a career. Continuous professional development should be provided throughout to maintain a high-quality tour and allow the guides to share best practice, keep up with the latest developments and constantly refresh and improve the experience they are delivering to visitors.

Table 9.3 *Visitor behaviour mitigations*

Visitor behaviour	Mitigation	Suggested example
Visitor touching an object they shouldn't	Verbally instruct the visitor, but in a way that explains why they shouldn't touch it, isn't too critical and is easy to link back to the tour.	'We actually don't touch that chair, and it's because it's a really important part of our collection. Let me tell you why . . .'
Visitors chatting during the tour	Ask the visitors a direct question to re-engage them.	'Why do you think . . . ?' 'Which is your favourite...?'
Visitors asking too many questions and holding up the tour for others	If this becomes excessive, suggest questions are kept to the end.	'There's so much I want to show you, so maybe if we do some questions at the end, I can spend a bit longer with you on that topic?'

Case Study 9: Hidden London, London Transport Museum

Tours of 'secret spaces' are always popular in London, and the semi-derelict areas of abandoned underground stations hold a special fascination for many. It's this unique sense of place that has driven the popularity of the London Transport Museum's 'Hidden London' tour programme. Since the 1990s, London Transport Museum has offered exclusive glimpses into London's hidden underground sites, exploring areas such as the deep-level World War 2 shelter at Clapham South and Churchill's 'secret station' at Down Street. Following investment from the Museum, and the appointment of a dedicated Hidden London tours manager, Oliver Burton, the programme has gone from strength to strength, attracting 30,000 visitors in 2019/20 (Burton, 2021).

It's undoubtedly the locations themselves that are the draw: the rich history of the sites as well as their hidden, exclusive nature. However, once on site, the tour experiences are shaped not by the stations but by the tour staff, who have the challenging task of bringing often bare and abandoned spaces back to life whilst also dealing with the many practical issues which come from being deep underground.

These issues mean that visitors' expectations have to be clearly set, and the team need to think ahead for the common pitfalls. 'For example, guests arriving with open-toed shoes are not allowed on the tour, so we keep sets of appropriate footwear to lend guests who despite our clear comms in advance, still occasionally turn up without the correct footwear' (Burton, 2021). They also need to plan ahead for any ill-health that might be caused by the conditions of the tour, such as claustrophobia or vertigo. As Burton explains, 'this is not common but does happen from time to time. In such circumstances we allow guests to take their time, and if necessary, take them back to the surface' (Burton, 2021).

When it comes to designing tours in some of these extremely challenging spaces, health and safety has to take priority. However, this challenge is also often turned into a positive on the tours. The hazardous nature of the environment helps visitors feel they are doing something out of the ordinary: giving them back that nature of surprise and excitement we discussed above. One of the requirements on some of the tours (for example when the group goes onto track) is that the staff wear high-visibility jackets. Again, the Hidden London team have turned this into a positive by getting all participants to wear hi-vis and hard hats, adding to the excitement and making the experience feel more real.

Underground, there is little freedom over the route taken. So, how can a narrative thread be found in space so dictated by infrastructure and engineering? 'It's all about telling the story of the site and its history,' says Burton. 'Our Engagement Manager who researches and writes the tours ensures that all the fascinating facts and history of the sites are woven into a logical and interesting tour route so guests come away feeling informed and entertained having spent time in these special, secret spaces. We use display panels, audio and sometimes video to punctuate the tour and link one stop to the next.'

When it comes to staffing, guides are recruited for the right skills and competencies. 'It's desirable that people have done tour guiding before, but it's not essential' says Burton. 'We look for people who are outgoing, engaging, great presentation skills, and have the ability to present information in an engaging way.' There are practical skills to consider as well; good operational sense and proactivity are needed to manage a tour in such a challenging environment. Some guides bring their own personal history of London transport; several guides are former or current Transport for London staff.

Full training is provided. 'There are two elements to the training. There's content training and there's delivery training', explains Burton. Content training involves a script, but as Burton pointed out 'they're not verbatim scripts that must be parroted', but rather a sheaf of comprehensive notes, which the guides are allowed paid time at home to fully digest before coming on site.

Then there's on-site training; shadowing, mock tours and of course the essential health and safety training. Some of this can be extremely in-depth: to be prepared to evacuate visitors effectively along train track at the Aldwych site, a guide requires a three-day Transport for London training course. And then, in order to deal with any challenging visitor behaviour, external trainers are brought in to brief the guides on conflict resolution. All-in-all, as Burton explains 'it's a pretty comprehensive end-to-end process to make sure they're ready.'

The experience also links directly to the Museum itself, with the two experiences branded very closely. At the end of each tour, the guide explains how ticket revenue from the Hidden London tours helps fund the museum's charitable aims and activities, and Hidden London visitors get discounted museum entry for a future visit. The end result is one of the most popular tour experiences in London, with visitors commenting positively, not just on the locations, which are undoubtedly unique, but on the experience the staff provide as well: 'This was one of the best things I have done in London. The staff were extremely knowledgeable and it was brilliant to see their enthusiasm. The station itself is so cloaked in history and so atmospheric' (Trip Advisor, 2021c).

CHAPTER 10

Crisis Management

> You can never guarantee who's going to be there on the day or the night of the incident.
>
> (Ann Fiddler, National Trust)

One area where Visitor Experience teams are always called to play a leading role is crisis management. In any unexpected incident, you'll find the knowledge of your team is crucial – as well as their practical experience of visitors, of the site and of what can be relied on to go wrong next! In this chapter, you'll find out how crisis management practice has developed in museums and heritage sites, how the COVID-19 pandemic has turned that all on its head and, most importantly, what you can do to prepare your teams for the crises of the future.

Crisis management in museums: a history

To understand how to plan for what might happen in the future, we first need to look to the past. This is because all crisis management is based on past experience.

Having grown up in 1990s Scotland, when I took my first London museum job I was fascinated by the stories of my long-established colleagues. In amongst the ghost stories and historic staff scandals were the memories of operating in the years when the Irish Republican Army (IRA) posed a clear and present threat in English cities. My colleagues told me tales of evacuations, bomb scares and coded warnings. These features were the warp and weft of the crises of the time, and we still see their legacy today in museum crisis management plans.

On 11 September 2001 our understanding of terrorism changed. Coded warnings and anonymous phone calls were the luxury of a previous era. Counter-terrorism focused on suicide bombers and mobile phone-detonated devices; and museums did not find themselves exempt from these concerns.

On 7 July 2005 bombers carried out an attack on the London transport network. However, at trial, the court heard that before the attack the perpetrators had also carried out hostile reconnaissance at a number of visitor attractions, including the London Eye and the Natural History Museum (Hough, 2008). We can take two lessons from this; first, that preventative measures put into place against hostile reconnaissance and terrorism are effective – because in this case, the bombers decided against those venues – and secondly, that with a propensity to draw large crowds and their status as cultural icons many museums and other visitor attractions were now definitely understood by terrorists as viable targets.

Museums adapted to the threat. This is the period that saw the widespread introduction of bag searching and other security procedures, with some attractions such as The View from the Shard and the House of Commons actually installing airport-style scanners and metal detectors. In the 2010s, there was further adaptation, this time due to the increased prevalence of 'lone-wolf' attacks. These attacks often utilised vehicles, following up with hand-held weapons like knives, machetes or even firearms. In the UK, one such attack on Westminster Bridge in March 2017 took the lives of five people, and prompted many visitor attractions to consider their vulnerability to vehicle attacks. Some city-centre attractions installed vehicle barriers to protect street queuing areas, and there was increased training for museum staff around escaping firearm or other handheld weapon attacks.

Although some of the procedures put in place as a result of these changes led to increased queues and wait times, visitors generally understood the safety benefits and many museums reported positive feedback from the public. More troubling was an increased feeling of racial profiling. A journal article from 2020 reported that in the last ten years British Muslims have increasingly reported feelings of being unwelcome in UK museums, due to the increased surveillance and suspicion focused on them (Atkinson, Yates and Brooke, 2020).

Even from this admittedly brief history, you can clearly see that when planning for crises we take stock of what is happening around us at the time. We learn from other countries and other organisations, and of course, we take advice from experts in the field.

The same is true of non-terror-related crises. The previous experience of fires at historic properties such as Hampton Court Palace in 1986 or Windsor Castle in 1992 have become embedded in heritage crisis management. In the recent COVID-19 crisis, it was clear that due to their previous experience of federal shutdowns, some organisations in the USA were more prepared for sudden temporary closures than their counterparts in other parts of the world. Kaywin Feldman, Director of the National Gallery of Art in Washington D. C. wrote:

> With several shutdowns in our history, the team at the National Gallery has a lot of expertise in temporarily closing the museum to the staff and public. We had already drafted our lists of staff positions and functions that are essential to daily operations when the facility is closed to the public.
>
> (Feldman, 2020)

Actually, we find the same idea of learning from experience as far back as World War 2. In the lead up to 1939, measures that had been put into place in a reactive way during World War 1 were part of the museum and heritage planning process, including moving the national collections out of London to protect them from bomb damage (Pearson, 2017). When the USA entered the conflict, they in turn looked to the UK so they could be informed by prior experience of heritage protection (Aiken, 2007, 275).

This rich history of crisis management in museums and heritage sites is a double-edged sword. On one hand, we have a huge back catalogue to draw on during times of crisis. This provides ideas, evidence of experience and a source of comfort when we recognise that other people have been through the same thing before. However, it also has a downside. With such a wealth of evidence highlighting the incidents we are most likely to experience – and in the UK over the last two decades this has been mainly localised incidents like fires, floods or even terrorist attacks – we run the risk of ignoring the possibility of crises we've never thought of.

If you can't imagine something happening, you can't plan for it. Therefore, the key to effective crisis management isn't planning for the expected; it's in preparing to deal with the unexpected.

Crisis management plans

When you are planning for crisis, it will probably come as no surprise that your Crisis Management Plan (CMP) should be a key weapon in your arsenal. Most museum and heritage organisations have one; and if yours doesn't, here are two things you can do to start the conversation.

First, as I've illustrated above, think about the history of your organisation. What type of crises has it experienced before? Are these things likely to happen again? Is the site located in a hurricane belt, a flood plain or another area that's prone to natural disasters or extreme weather? A good way of making these judgements is to put together a Risk Register; a document which lists possible risks to your organisation based on how likely they are to happen, and the severity of their impact. When you're doing this, don't forget to consider the unexpected. The most challenging incidents will often be the ones that haven't happened to us before. Just putting together your Risk Register will help you start to think about planning for these events.

Secondly, ask your colleagues across the sector (and other sectors too) if you can have a look at their CMPs. Many templates can be transferable, and there's no point in reinventing the wheel if you don't have to. Obviously, plans need to be specific to the organisation in question, but sometimes it's useful to have a format to get you thinking about what you need. Figure 10.1 is a basic contents list to get you started.

1	**Document Control** 1.1 Amendment Log 1.2 Distribution 1.3 Review	9	**Action in the Event of an Explosion** 9.1 General Principles 9.2 Manager Response
2	**Types of Crises**	10	**Breach of Security** 10.1 General Principles 10.2 Location of Security Panel 10.3 Staff Response 10.4 Contact Details
3	**General Crisis Guidelines** 3.1 Crisis Management Team 3.2 Emergency Services 3.3 Media Plan 3.4 Handovers and Standing Down 3.5 Business Continuity	11	**IT Incidents** 11.1 Location of Services
4	**Evacuations** 4.1 Location of Fire Panel 4.2 Evacuation Procedures	12	**Power Failure** 12.1 Staff Response 12.2 Supply Details 12.3 Gas Leak
5	**Medical Emergency** 5.1 Staff Response 5.2 First Aid Resources	13	**Loss of Water Supply/Leaks and Floods** 13.1 Staff Response 13.2 Supplier Details
6	**Suspect Devices** 6.1 Recognition 6.2 Staff Response	14	**External Crises Requiring Organisational Shutdown**
7	**Suspect Letter/Postal Bomb** 7.1 Recognition 7.2 Staff Response	**Appendix 1**	**Incident Review Report**
8	**Telephone Bomb Warning** 8.1 General Principles 8.2 Staff Response		

Figure 10.1 *Crisis management plan: suggested contents*

If you already have a CMP, is it still fit for purpose? What is your plan trying to achieve? Does it provide a framework for the decision-making process of the Crisis Management Team, or is it a step-by-step guide of what to do in any given situation? Generally, plans tend to fall into one camp or another (Ferraro and Henderson, 2011). Either they talk about the people that are going to make certain decisions, and the framework in which those decisions will be made; or they give detailed instructions on how to deal with a variety of different situations. Both of these approaches have their merits. Focusing on explicit instructions means that in theory, anyone can pick up the plan and run with it. But trying to predict every possible incident means that such a plan will likely run incredibly long and, in my experience, it's almost certain that when crisis does strike, it'll be the one thing people never thought of. For example, in a recent survey, 48% of operational staff in UK museum and heritage sites said that a pandemic was not included in their organisations' CMPs prior to COVID-19 (Mackay, 2020b). On the other hand, not including any of this information and only focusing on decision-making frameworks means that you are relying heavily on the knowledge and experience of a few individuals. If they weren't around (which, in a crisis, is not beyond the realms of possibility), would anyone know what decisions to make?

For me, a happy compromise comes from balancing both sides. Include instructions on how to deal with some of the most common crises, and certainly think through the main processes and procedures for a major incident, including liaising with emergency services. But don't spend too much time trying to predict every possible incident. It's more critical to identify the roles that are needed in the Crisis Management Team (such as liaising with staff, local government or the media) and setting out the processes for contacting critical teams like maintenance, conservation or salvage. Your goal should be a CMP which is comprehensive enough to be of practical use, but flexible enough to accommodate decision making around a crisis you haven't predicted yet.

Remember that not every crisis has a defined beginning and end. Many existing CMPs are divided into Emergency Management and Business Continuity sections. For example, if there was a fire at your attraction, the Emergency Management section would deal with putting out the fire and evacuating people to safety, and the Business Continuity section would focus on getting the business up and running again. This is another area of crisis management that COVID-19 has turned on its head. When a pandemic has no defined end or beginning, and no clear or fixed lines between the crisis and the continuity, do these formats still work? With this in mind, it might be worth adopting a more fluid approach when writing or updating your plan.

Museums and heritage organisations usually identify a Crisis Management Team, who are responsible for putting together the plan and utilising it when needed. There will also usually be one member of that team who 'owns' the plan and is responsible for the actual writing and updating. Often, this will be a senior member of the Visitor Experience or Operations team. This makes practical sense; however, it's important to ensure that there is plenty of collaboration going into the creation of a CMP. If the plan is developed by one person only, it is very likely to be read by one person only. The whole organisation needs to be aware of the plan, and be willing and able to follow its contents when needed. The best way to ensure this sort of buy-in is to make sure all members of staff feel involved in its creation.

In addition to buy-in, collaboration is the way to gather the critical information needed for building a CMP. It's only by discussing different crisis scenarios with various departments that you'll get a good idea of how incidents might affect them, and what resources they might have at their disposal. For example, how might a transport infrastructure problem impact the stock of your retail team? Or, to use a real-world example, how many of us knew that our Conservation colleagues used PPE before museums donated stocks of protective equipment to key workers during the COVID-19 pandemic (Shaw, 2020)? Similarly, some of your colleagues in other departments might not have the same understanding as you about the impacts of crisis on visitors; how long it takes to evacuate, for example, or what your ticketing system can cope with in terms of refunds. Information like this can help you think through all the different impacts that crises will have, and ultimately build a CMP to fit. So, no matter how tempting it might be to lock yourself away in a room and just get the plan written, make sure you're bringing in as many different voices as possible.

Once your plan is written, it's never really finished. A CMP is a living document, and needs constant attention. Firstly, it will need updating often. In the museum and heritage world, things change all the time, from organisational structures to the names of buildings and rooms, so put regular updates in your diary to keep the plan fresh and relevant.

Secondly, it needs to be used. Crisis Management skills are like muscles; if you don't use them often, they won't be there when you really need them. I would recommend regular table-top exercises with your team, at least once a quarter. Devise some scenarios and talk through them, using your CMP as a guide. I've included an example in Table 10.1 to get you started.

Table 10.1 *Crisis management training scenario*

Scenario	It's Friday, and you have a wedding for 150 people booked in for tomorrow. Your historic building is located near an area of open grassland, and it's been a long, hot, dry summer. The news reports that a wildfire has started in the grassland. Fire crews are dealing with it, and the fire is currently about 30 miles from your site. What do you do?
Progression 1	It's Saturday morning and people are beginning to set up for the wedding. However, the fire is still going, and now it is only 20 miles away. You are closed to the public for the wedding anyway, but guests will be arriving in a couple of hours. What do you do?
Progression 2	It's 12.00. The fire service give the order to evacuate your site. What decisions must you make now?

Table-top exercises are a great way to test your plan. What issues arise? What haven't you thought about before? Does the plan need to be updated as a result? You'll find that every scenario you practise leads to a new realisation. It's also a good way to get into the habit of making those critical decisions under pressure. Even if the scenario is something that is extremely unlikely to happen, like an alien invasion or a haunting (not that unlikely at Hampton Court Palace!), it's the flexing of those muscles that is important.

Finally, don't forget to review your plan after every incident. In fact, I would recommend including a blank review form in the appendices to your plan to prompt immediate review. In one of the museums I worked in, we would bring everyone together for a 'wash-up' meeting as soon as possible – usually the same day. It's important that you collect everyone's experiences of what worked and what didn't during these real incidents, because (happily) the opportunities for such learning are usually rare.

Endless practice and constant review, then, are the two things that will turn your CMP from another folder gathering dust on a shelf into the key to managing crises successfully.

Leadership and communication in a crisis

Leadership of and communication with our teams is never more important than during a crisis. During the COVID-19 pandemic, research shows that operations managers at UK museum and heritage sites felt that internal communication was a bigger challenge than external communication (Mackay, 2020c). There were two major issues; first, that information was so sparse that leaders felt they didn't have enough to pass on to their teams; and secondly, when information did come out, decisions were made so quickly that there wasn't enough time to update everyone fully on what was happening (for example, furlough or reopening) (Mackay, 2020c).

These issues might feel specific to COVID-19, but they aren't. Communication is often a challenge, because many crises are characterised by a lack of clarity about what is happening now, and what is likely to happen next. Against this uncertain backdrop, strong leadership is crucial. This doesn't necessarily mean an authoritarian approach. Instead, visibility, authenticity and clear decision making are the themes that arise time and time again in case studies as being the desirable attributes of a leader in crisis (Mackay, 2020c).

What COVID-19 did show us was that crises can last a lot longer than we had previously thought. When we used to talk about managing crises, we were mainly talking about incidents that lasted a day or less, and when we talk about communication in that context, there's not too much planning to be done. Instructions are given and followed. Communication is practical and brief. During COVID-19, with all the separation and isolation that came along with the pandemic, we all became much more aware of the value of longer-term communication. We saw teams using new channels and technologies to communicate, not just for business-critical updates, but for social contact. Communications trees and weekly check-ins were hurriedly arranged. Zoom quizzes were won and lost. This is an aspect of crisis communication that we hadn't seen before, and one that has prompted many organisations to give this area more attention in their CMPs.

Before getting too prescriptive, though, it might be wise to recognise that many of those social channels that functioned so well during the pandemic were home-grown. Whilst some managers despaired that they didn't have the right systems in place to reach everyone at the same time, others were happier with a more organic approach, asking staff which channels they were more comfortable with, and letting social groups grow naturally without too much interference from senior staff (Mackay, 2020c). The success of this approach, however, hinges on knowing your organisation and being able to trust that people are not falling through the cracks. In other words, an organisation that communicates well outside crisis is best placed to communicate well during crisis. So, put in all that groundwork now, before a crisis happens.

Case Study 10: Fire at Osborne House

Even better than the table-top crisis exercises described earlier are live exercises involving multiple stakeholders, including the emergency services. Fair warning: doing something like this takes a lot of work. However, I think this case study from Osborne House, managed by English Heritage (EH), demonstrates exactly why they can be so valuable.

Osborne House is the beautiful summer palace of Queen Victoria, situated on the Isle of Wight. Its location brings certain challenges when it comes to crisis management. The island fire service only has four emergency trucks, so if there is a major fire, help needs to be sought from Hampshire Fire and Rescue Service on the mainland. This means obvious delays when it comes to fighting a fire, a concern that Operations Manager Ann Fiddler was not unaware of when she took up her post in 2014 (Fiddler, 2022). Then, an emergency elsewhere really focused her mind.

'The following year, the Clandon Park [National Trust] fire happened' Fiddler explains. 'That to me was just a real eye-opener. EH were already reviewing a lot of their emergency procedures and it just really highlighted my responsibilities and what I needed to do'. Following the fire, the Trust put lots of information and films online, and Fiddler learned that the Clandon Park team had performed a salvage exercise just weeks before the incident, 'which is why they were so on top of it. And the independent military museum that was next to it lost everything because they had no procedures; they hadn't practised.'

Fiddler was thinking about how best to revise procedures and refresh training when coincidentally, a representative from Hampshire Fire and Rescue Service visited Osborne. During the visit, Fiddler was asked if she wanted to take part in a joint salvage exercise. The proposed exercise would have five main objectives:

- to test the Osborne House emergency procedures and protocols
- to simulate a multi-agency response to a high-priority national heritage site
- to evaluate assistance and support from mainland resources
- to test and evaluate the salvage and removal of high- and special-value items from a historical residence
- to test on-site water supplies and communications.

With only a few weeks to go until the proposed exercise, Fiddler began getting the internal support and resources she needed in place. 'EH has a whole department for looking at fire safety, so I got that team involved, and started getting visits from them to start working out what had happened previously in EH. I had been sent several useful documents but it was quite clear it had been quite a few years since EH had done anything on this scale: certainly nothing had ever been done at Osborne before.'

The wider working group, made of the emergency services and EH representatives, realised straightaway that they would need to involve a ferry company. 'Interestingly, they have no legal responsibility to help emergency services get to the island; it's all done by local agreement. We soon got the Operations Manager from Red Funnel [one of the ferry companies that serves the Isle of Wight] involved. So they pre-booked those ferries out that we needed, basically to be filled up with the fire engines, which made quite a spectacle for the other passengers involved!'

To further prepare herself for what the exercise at Osborne would be like, Fiddler visited Beaulieu Abbey to watch a salvage exercise there. 'I was able to see that team in action using things like book slides out of the window; really interesting to see that all happen and how it might unfold at Osborne.'

Back on site, Fiddler began a programme of staff training. 'Every two weeks we did training early in the morning so people could still go on and open up as normal, where we'd give them breakfast and then deliver some training, whether it was collections handling or a tour round the various wings, looking at those priority items' Fiddler explains. 'Then, as we got closer to September it was more focused around the exercise and how it was going to run.'

The EH team wanted to keep Osborne House open to the public whilst the exercise was going on. In order to not intrude on the visitor experience, a suite of unused rooms was chosen. 'We dressed those rooms with pretend stuff' explains Fiddler. 'Some of us went round various charity shops and just got stuff that was "collection", found random copies of pictures of Queen Victoria . . . basically, dressed them as if they were show rooms and that became the practice suite for getting the team used to how we would handle objects and what we would do.'

When the day finally came, 'we had set up with the fire brigade and police to ring in a real 999 call. So, everything went through the system as it would do normally'. Then, as the scenario they had created beforehand played out, 'the incident keeps getting upgraded and eventually is declared a major incident.' Fiddler says they even pretended that the security officer who first went to check on smoke reports had gone missing! 'That was something the fire brigade very much wanted to test; sending their officers into smoke. They didn't put smoke in there because obviously we didn't want the real collection to get affected, so what they did was stick on a blocker on their visor so that it looked like they were going into a smoke-filled room.'

And did visitors mind watching the fire brigade carry out pretend bits of salvage all day? Quite to the contrary, Fiddler says. 'Visitors loved it. Absolutely loved it!'

Fiddler says the opportunity to see the fire brigade at work at their site was invaluable. 'It's only through testing and working with them that you work out what works.' For the fire brigade, a critical lesson was learned between the Hampshire and Isle of Wight Fire and Rescue services. 'Their radios didn't work with each other!' Fiddler exclaims. 'So, they were then having to rely on personal mobile phones to talk to each other.' Luckily, this problem was identified and corrected before a large fire in Cowes, on the Isle of Wight, the following year, which also necessitated engines being brought over from the mainland.

EH also learned some really valuable lessons. 'I sent out surveys,' says Fiddler, 'and we had a number of observers on site to watch what was happening and feed back. They gave us really positive feedback. We had 130 items which were all retrieved in less than an hour.' There were also some useful pointers about what to work on for the future. 'Certainly, some of our documentation processes were just too much, over the top, the number of times we were having to document in various different stages was just unnecessary in an emergency.'

The exercise was also a useful opportunity to carry out some cross-training. Each person who played a role in the exercise was being shadowed by another member of the team. 'You can never guarantee who's going to be there on the day or the night of the incident, so it's about people seeing it happening and then building up their confidence.'

All in all, the exercise was invaluable in giving the on-site salvage team an idea of what a real emergency would look like, and what they would be required to do. 'Seeing it happen gave them more confidence,' said Fiddler. 'When you work in a house where you can't touch things and then all of a sudden, you're being told to lift them, it can be quite daunting, so that's where the practice with the collections specialists on how to lift and carry certain objects really helped.'

This is a great example of a crisis exercise, because not only were the EH team able to realistically simulate what would happen in an emergency, they built relationships with the organisations and emergency services they would need to rely on in a real crisis. But it doesn't need to be as huge an undertaking as this. Why not reach out to your local emergency services and discuss what practice you could do together?

The more realistic we can make crisis exercises, the better prepared your team will be. It's not about getting everything right first time, it's about practically testing out the theory of the Crisis Management Plans, and most importantly, using those critical decision-making skills.

PART 3

Developing the Visitor Experience

In my experience, most people who have a passion for this sector don't want to merely manage the status quo. We are constantly looking to evolve and develop the experiences we deliver, adapting and flexing to meet changing needs and trying new things to engage our visitors in different ways. Therefore, this final section of the book looks at the skills and tools we need to do exactly that.

As Visitor Experience professionals, we rarely work in silos. We have interdependencies with other departments, and must work with others to best serve the visitors. Therefore, if we want to develop and evolve our experiences, we must also become advocates for them. Chapter 11 explores different methods of doing this, with a case study from the Mary Rose Museum to show these methods in practice.

In order to develop our experiences, we must first have an accurate picture of the current reality, and a way of measuring our development as we progress. Chapter 12 therefore explores different methods for measuring the quality of the visitor experience, highlighting a blended approach from the Natural History Museum to show that there is no one-size-fits all solution when it comes to visitor evaluation.

'Creating a Visitor Experience Strategy', which is the title of Chapter 13, may sound as though it's only relevant to national museums who develop and deliver all sorts of big 'strategies' on a regular basis. However, a Visitor Experience Strategy can be as simple as making a quick but bold decision about what audience you serve and how you do it, as the case study from the community-focused London Museum of Water and Steam will show.

Continuing development and engagement of your Visitor Experience team is absolutely critical to the development of the visitor experience. Without a team that is consistently engaged and learning, you will struggle to keep the experiences you deliver fresh. Chapter 14 examines continuing employee engagement and training programmes, whilst Chapter 15 explores how a culture of innovation can be fostered within your team.

Finally, all of these approaches will mean change for your team and your organisation, so it seemed only fitting to finish with a chapter, Chapter 16, exploring change management strategies and how they fit within the Visitor Experience context.

CHAPTER 11

Advocating for the Visitor Experience

> Visitor feedback is the key thing.
>
> (Paul Griffiths, Painshill Park)

In talking with colleagues in the Visitor Experience world, both in general and in researching this book, I have run into a common challenge: common enough to focus a chapter on it here. This section of the book is all about developing the visitor experience: setting new goals and taking your operation forward to achieve them. To do that, it's really important that within our organisations we act as effective advocates for the visitor experience, working alongside colleagues in other departments to deliver visitor-centred improvements.

And yet this isn't always as simple as it sounds. Through conversations with others and my own experience, I know that there can often be barriers to effective advocacy. In this chapter, we'll look at some of these barriers and explore examples of best practice from across the sector to learn how to overcome them.

Barriers to effective advocacy

One of the most common barriers to visitor experience advocacy is the positioning of the responsible department within the organisation. The name given to what I would call the Visitor Experience team changes over time and across different organisations, as does where the department sits. I have seen it included as part of a wider Operations team, part of the Public Engagement team, part of the Learning team, part of the Marketing and Audience Development team, part of the Commercial team: the list is endless. You might think this doesn't matter: Visitor Experience teams have to work with everyone in the organisation to deliver the visitor offer, so what does it matter where they sit?

Actually, I've found that it really does make a difference. In small or big museums, having a senior champion of visitor experience, whether that's through management structure or through having a senior advocate at board level, will hugely impact how visitor-centric your organisation is, and how seriously the job of those in visitor-facing roles is taken. Job titles and organograms matter. If that sounds far-fetched, consider this example from someone I interviewed for this book (who I will keep anonymous for obvious reasons). This person told me the story of working in a large organisation where the operations team were called 'custodians', whilst other teams were known as the 'professional' staff. The professional staff even had a nickname for the staff on site: 'donkeys'. As my source commented: 'God, that wound me up. Everyone is professional!'

This story took place some time ago, and I'm happy to say that, generally, things have moved on. Unfortunately, however, there are still some isolated examples across the sector where Visitor Experience is considered to be less of a specialism than other museum professions. I've certainly had experiences myself where I've felt I needed to get the backing of external consultants in order to have my views heard. As frustrating as this can be, I think that the onus is on us Visitor Experience professionals to get our voices and specialist knowledge heard and listened to. Although it can be tempting to just blame organisational structure or culture, and give up, it might be more useful to consider how we can be such effective advocates that we cement our credibility and change the culture around us.

Visitor research experts Ben Gammon and Jo Graham offer an interesting insight into this from their work at the Science Museum. In their article, they identify several barriers to effective audience advocacy, such as management structure, stakeholder involvement and late evaluation. However, the authors also pose a new challenge: 'Nobody has asked whether we the audience advocates are communicating effectively with our audience. Curators are people too, you know' (Gammon and Graham, 1998, 6). Although as Visitor Experience professionals we consider each communication with visitors extremely carefully, do we always put the same thought into how we communicate with our internal stakeholders?

For example, Gammon and Graham use the example of sending through frequent, unwieldy visitor feedback reports and expecting internal teams to engage. 'In our experience,' they say, 'the failure of exhibition teams to act on the advice of audience advocates is not necessarily due to their lack of interest or willingness, but because we are asking them to do what we would never expect out visitors to do – read, memorise and draw conclusions from vast quantities of text' (Gammon and Graham, 1998, 6). Later in the chapter, we'll explore how we can deliver visitor awareness in different ways, but for now

I think it's important to acknowledge that not all of the barriers come from others not listening: sometimes it's about how we ourselves communicate.

The final barrier to effective Visitor Experience advocacy goes to the very root of the most basic philosophical question: what should a museum be? John Falk describes this in his article 'Museum Audiences: a visitor-centred perspective'. Talking about the age-old debate between the academic/conservation role and the public role of museums, he says 'the debate around this question has often been shrill with much of the discussion simplistically framed as a dichotomy between "quality/education" and "quantity/entertainment"' (Falk, 2016, 357). This argument can mean that when advocating for the needs of the visitor, we can face accusations of dumbing down 'content in order to appeal to the masses' and therefore sell tickets, or attract more visitors. It's certainly an argument I am familiar with, as, I suspect are many of you in Visitor Experience.

However, Falk argues that this is the wrong debate. Both sides of the argument, he says, represent a 'museum-centric' mindset, one academic and one commercial. Instead, we should be aiming for a visitor-centric approach:

> The visitor-centred perspective focuses on the users of museums – both current and potential; individuals who have no enduring financial or personal stake in the museum. It asks the question what is the perceived value of the museum to these individuals, those who visit and those who do not. In taking this perspective, the question becomes more about satisfaction than 'outcomes'.
>
> (Falk, 2016, 357)

How do we deliver this visitor-centred focus in practice? Let's look at some great advocacy examples from across the sector, and from all the different areas of museum work.

Positive lessons in advocacy

1. Audience Advocates at the Science Museum

One way the Science Museum has attempted to ensure that the visitor experience is considered throughout project delivery is to use designated roles called 'Audience Advocates'. The advocate role exists on all major projects and acts as adviser, assessor, strategist, trainer and evaluator. The role is financed through the evaluation budget, and front-end and summative evaluation is a big part of the job description, but it isn't just about research. For example, when the Science Museum was developing the new 'Who Am I?' gallery, the Audience Advocate undertook training with the project team to help them remember what it was like to be a visitor (Burch, 2013). In this way, colleagues can be moved towards that 'visitor-centric' perspective that Falk describes.

The Audience Advocate role is exactly what Ben Gammon and Jo Graham suggest as their solution to the delivery problem mentioned earlier (Gammon and Graham, 1998). As Audience Advocates at the Science Museum, they came up with a new training programme, designed to engage colleagues with the visitor mindset in an interactive and dynamic way. Rather than giving them reams of data to read, they developed four exercises under a programme called 'Inside the Visitor's Head'. Gammon and Graham say:

> . . . we wanted to provide something more motivating, compelling, and infinitely more memorable than just a great big wordy document. We also wanted to establish our credibility with the team by allowing them to see for themselves what visitors do, think, feel and say.
>
> (Gammon and Graham, 1998, 7)

The exercises were as follows (Gammon and Graham, 1998):

- 'A Day at the Museum': an accompanied visit with various questions answered along the way. (You can find out more about accompanied visits in the next chapter.)
- 'Have a Bad Day': give colleagues the experience of being 'an extremely reluctant visitor'. Ask them to visit a museum they do not want to go to, and complete pre- and post-visit questionnaires.
- 'Insect Visitors': Visitor observations, spending 45 minutes in one location. 'In order to focus their attention, we asked participants to imagine that they were classifying each visitor as a kind of insect. Are they grasshoppers leaping quickly from one thing to another? Army ants moving in columns destroying all in their path? Bees moving methodically and purposefully through the area? Or are they stick insects – you have to look really hard to see them move?'
- 'Coffee Mornings': optional informal weekly meetings on different specialist topics.

How could you utilise some of these exercises at your museum?

2. Design sprints at the British Museum

'Design sprints' will be familiar to those who have worked in digital teams and in fact this example does come from the digital team at the British Museum (BM). Put simply, a design sprint is a short period of time when all other work is put aside to design, test and learn from a prototype in order to solve a problem. In this scenario, the digital team were looking at how the website could best support wayfinding in the Museum. To assist with this, they trialled several products on site to learn from visitor reactions.

However, it was the process rather than the products themselves that were important to the digital team. Dana Mitroff Silvers, writing up the experiment for *Design Thinking for Museums*, explains: 'Instead of trying to sell the rest of the Museum on the new disciplines of product management and user experience design, [the BM team] used a sprint as a way to demonstrate their process and approach' (Mitroff Silvers, 2016). This 'hidden agenda' also showed colleagues how to participate in a more visitor-centred approach, valuing visitor data over personal opinion.

For example, one experiment involved creating a sign that said 'Can I help?' and holding it up in the Great Court. Whilst some staff assumed the holder would get all sorts of questions about the collection, the majority of questions related to wayfinding. 'There were lots of questions about the coat check and bathrooms!'

In this example, internal colleagues benefited from seeing visitor responses for themselves, and updated their own views on visitor behaviour by taking part in a user-centred process.

3. A change in culture at de Havilland Aircraft Museum

Obviously, not every museum is the Science Museum or the British Museum. So how do smaller museums champion the visitor within their teams?

John Baldwin, Trustee at the de Havilland Aircraft Museum in Hertfordshire, has been present at the Museum through an intense period of change. A few years ago, the visitor profile of de Havilland, which is the home of the iconic wartime plane the de Havilland Mosquito, was very much Falk's 'professional/enthusiast' (see Chapter 4). Visitors would have a specific interest in particular planes, and many of the museum's volunteers were retired aircraft engineers. Their primary motive in volunteering was to continue working on planes rather than engaging visitors. However, aeroplanes also do well at attracting a family audience, and it became clear to the de Havilland team that to ensure their long-term sustainability, they needed to focus more on the visitor experience, and move away from the model that Baldwin affectionately calls 'men in sheds' (Baldwin, 2022).

Part of this refocus has involved more cross-working, so that it's not just the stewards, but also the volunteers working on restoration projects, who get close contact with the visitors. Volunteers also take on compiling and analysing annual visitor survey results, so that they get a well-rounded understanding of how visitors feel and what they are saying. Volunteers have been given more autonomy. They can prepare their own interpretation for aircraft they are working on, and can make decisions around practical things like the visitor route and lighting. This means that not only is decision-making simplified in what is a small museum with limited resources, but volunteers have to be constantly thinking about the impact of their decisions on visitors.

Baldwin says the change in focus hasn't been easy. 'There is pushback,' he says, explaining that there are times that volunteers just want to talk about their own specialist subject without considering the interests of the visitor. However, internal champions for the visitor experience provide strong leadership in this area; trying to get the whole organisation into the habit of considering things from the visitor point of view. There is now broad recognition that it's all about the visitor, and planned future investment in training and development of visitor-facing staff and volunteers.

Learning lessons

Looking at the above examples of positive advocacy, some key themes emerge:

- engage your colleagues (think as carefully about communication with them as you would do with visitors)
- build credibility (an evidence-based approach, using robust visitor research where possible)
- put colleagues in the visitors' shoes and encourage them to come up with their own solutions.

So how can we bring these themes to the advocacy role that is part of our daily work in Visitor Experience?

Back-to-the-floor schemes

I'm a huge fan of back-to-the-floor schemes wherever I find them. I heard once that at McDonalds, no matter if you are in Marketing, or Finance, or whether you're the CEO, you have to spend your first week working in the restaurant. I have no idea whether that's true or not, but I hope it is. When the whole point of an organisation is to deliver a visitor-facing experience, every member of the company should have direct knowledge of that role. When you think about it, that's even more true of visitor attractions.

I introduced a scheme like this when I was at the Natural History Museum (NHM), called the Visitor Experience Support Team, or VEST. During busy periods, the Visitor Experience teams invited colleagues from back of house to come and spend a couple of hours on the floor assisting visitors. They were given a short training course, a sash that identified them as being 'Here to help' and a location that was a key orientation point but wouldn't need any complex training, such as till points or queue management. We sold it as a plea to come and help the team on the floor during our really busy days (and it was), but it also had a deeper purpose: advocacy. Getting back-of-house staff to spend some time with visitors really helped them understand the operational issues on the floor, and understand what visitors were looking for. We asked all directors to take part, and I'll never forget going to pick one of them up after their shift. 'It really is just about dinosaurs and toilets, isn't it?' they said, wonderingly. 'Yep,' I nodded. 'Dinosaurs and toilets. That's the NHM in a nutshell.'

That's not to say, of course, that all visitors get from the Natural History Museum is dinosaurs and toilets. But it's no use trying to engage visitors in climate change when they've just got through the main entrance and are desperate for the loo! We have to meet people's most pressing needs before we get into the deep stuff.

I stole VEST from the British Museum, by the way. None of these ideas need to be original. Take what you like and make it work for your organisation.

In my view, all trustees and directors should spend some time on the floor; it would certainly make advocating for the visitor experience so much easier. Just look at what British Museum Trustee Mary Beard learnt from her stint in the Front-of-House team:

> It was hugely good fun, but more than a stunt. For a start it gave me a chance to find out what that job was like (completely knackering, but also much less 'warder-ish' than I imagined . . . my instructions insisted that while I was there for security, I was also there to make visitors feel welcome and answer questions). But it also gave me an opportunity to study what visitors actually *do* in a museum gallery (it's hard to do that when you are a visitor yourself without appearing to be snooping).
>
> (Beard, 2020)

Getting those in power to see for themselves how visitors act and behave isn't just advocacy by stealth: it's the best sort of advocacy there is.

Legwork, evidence, co-ordinate

Not every problem can be solved just by observing visitors. Sometimes you will have a goal or a project in mind that means you need to win the support of others in your organisation. When I reflect on what has worked for me in the past, I think of a three-stage process that encompasses legwork, evidence and co-ordination. I'll use an example from Historic Royal Palaces to elaborate.

1. Legwork

Advocacy is a journey, and this first stage, particularly, takes a lot of energy. When I was at Kew Palace, a few of us within the organisation really wanted our story to focus on King George III's mental health story from a contemporary perspective (as discussed in Chapter 8). However, as an organisation, we hadn't done anything of that type at Kew before, and we hadn't put contemporary objects on display as we would eventually do in 'George III: The Mind Behind the Myth'. At Historic Royal Palaces, functions such as Interpretation, Conservation and Communities work centrally, rather than at individual sites. This means staff are all really busy delivering projects and work across six Palaces. To deliver this project at Kew, all of those teams had to be involved. The first step was to do the legwork. Luckily, there were some key allies across the organisation who shared the same vision. Many of the people we needed to talk to were based at other Palaces, so we had to walk the corridors, attend as any meetings as possible, catch people before and after meetings, pop into offices and try to infect everyone with our enthusiasm for the project. For me, it really helped that I was already a volunteer with the suicide prevention charity CALM, so some of the important facts and figures around the importance of mental wellbeing were already at the top of my mind.

2. Evidence

Next, we worked with members of our public engagement teams to deliver a couple of mini-events that would provide evidence that this idea could work. First, we used my connections with CALM to run a week of activity during our off-season, including mindfulness activities, tours and crafts. We reached a relatively small number of people, but the feedback was so powerful that we could see a longer-running programme would have real value for visitors. Then, the Kew team worked with our brilliant cross-organisation Communities team to host an open evening for local charities and organisations to come in, go on some guided tours and tell us what was important to them. That way, we gained evidence as to what Kew Palace could support the local community with when it came to mental health.

3. Co-ordination

Once the project was in motion, I saw my specific role as one of co-ordination: the person who checked that all the plates were spinning in the different teams and made sure everything was still on track. Whilst exhibition delivery teams were busy producing our amazing displays, I was envisioning the visitor journey, thinking about support for our Host team and trying to problem-solve in advance. This last stage is just as important as the ones before: through effective co-ordination you continue your advocacy by making sure everyone stays on track, and that the visitor remains at the centre of every decision made.

Hopefully that example shows how following a process of legwork, evidence and co-ordination can work in practice and how you can apply a similar process in your own organisation. A word of warning though: advocacy isn't necessarily easy and it is never short. From conception to delivery of the Kew project took over four years – although at least part of that delay was because of COVID-19. My point is that it's a marathon, not a sprint, so try to think of advocacy as a part of your everyday job, rather than something you do once and then never have to do again. Championing the visitor experience is continuous.

Case Study 11: Advocacy and change at the Mary Rose Museum

This case study explores how advocating for the visitor experience can drive changes, even to a brand-new museum.

Paul Griffiths was brought in as Head of Operations at the Mary Rose Museum in Portsmouth in 2012. Like the rest of the Operations team, he arrived after the new museum, which opened in May 2013, had already been designed. This meant that, without a key person to advocate for the visitor experience, not everything about the new museum worked flawlessly (Griffiths, 2021).

For example, the operation had launched with timed tickets to help manage capacity. Whilst this was no doubt a sensible move, there hadn't been certainty about what the dwell time would be. 'People were going in not realising they were going to be in there two or three hours' Griffiths says. Then, when they did want to leave, the dark, immersive environment architects had created didn't lend itself to wayfinding. So, when visitors realised they had been there longer than intended and did have to leave '. . . they couldn't get out because it was dark and there was no obvious exit route.'

Another issue was the retail experience. In a scenario familiar to many operators, the shop had been designed by architects rather than retail experts. Full of low-level counters, with nothing at eye level, the shop just wasn't appealing to visitors or delivering the income that had been forecast.

These issues are problematic for any operation, but after a multi-million-pound relaunch, the appetite for further investment was low. Griffiths describes one of his biggest challenges as 'convincing our CEO at the time that he needed to spend loads more money, when he'd just spent £35 million on a brand-new museum which had been designed by one of the most highly respected architects.'

How did Griffiths advocate for the changes visitors needed? In order to influence internal colleagues, he did the legwork and gathered support and advice from across the sector: 'From a retail perspective, we spoke to all sorts of retail experts, and we looked at best practice constantly' he explains. 'It was always about looking and then presenting back and saying, look, we've been to X, and this is what their shop looks like, and this is what they're delivering in spend per head.' Griffiths credits the sector for always being so quick to collude in what he jokingly refers to as 'industrial espionage'. 'People are so nice, so keen to share.'

To drive changes in wayfinding, Griffiths gathered evidence from the Museum's visitors. 'We used a lot of survey data, we were getting something like 100 forms done a week, so we were using that data', he explains. 'Visitor feedback was the key thing.' Like Gammon and Graham at the Science Museum, however, Griffiths quickly realised that just handing over pages and pages of data wasn't going to engage his colleagues. Instead, he sorted comments into Post-it notes, colour-coding them by theme. By presenting them in this way, colleagues could see at a glance that signage and wayfinding was a key challenge for visitors: 'They got it instantly.' Changes were made, and clearer wayfinding signage introduced. Visitor feedback was also used to help phase out timed tickets, and make the purchasing part of the visitor journey clearer.

Therefore, by going through those three phases; doing the legwork of learning from other organisations, gathering evidence from visitor feedback and co-ordinating a response from the management team, Griffiths was able to advocate for the visitor and improve the overall experience.

Now, as Director of the historic Painshill Park in Surrey, Griffiths agrees that effective advocacy often depends on where Visitor Experience is positioned in the organisation. It's important to 'have those advocates for the visitor experience at the centre of the organisation' he says. 'Today, as Director, with my operations background, we have a Visitor Experience-focused lead for the organisation.'

CHAPTER 12

Measuring the Visitor Experience

> What works for visitors? What doesn't work? How could we make it better?
>
> (Emma Morioka)

This part of the book is focusing on developing the visitor experience; in other words, assessing current performance, identifying ways of improvement and managing your teams and your resources to get you there. The first step of this undertaking has to be measuring the visitor experience you are delivering now. This chapter discusses some of the methods that might be used to gain such a measurement, and how the data you gather can be used to inform the way forward.

Museum evaluation

Measuring the quality of visitor experience is one part of the much bigger topic of museum evaluation, an area of research that has grown considerably in the last 20 years. In some cases, this has been driven by the requirements of funders such as the National Lottery Heritage Fund as they ensure that key goals are being met, but also by our increasing desire as museum professionals to ensure we are staying relevant to our audiences' needs. This includes measuring the visitor experience.

If you want to learn about museum evaluation more broadly, the Association of Independent Museums (AIM), Museums Galleries Scotland (MGS) and The Audience Agency (2021a) all have great free online resources. You can find links at the end of the book. For now, because museum evaluation is such a broad topic and we will be focusing on a relatively narrow section of it here, I thought it would be useful to provide a quick description of some of the terms commonly used:

- **Primary research:** This is direct research, straight from visitors to you.
- **Secondary research:** This is often desk-based research, using secondary sources such as historic evaluation data.
- **Quantitative research:** This type of research looks for data that can be expressed in numbers. It is great for measuring how many, or how much, but less good at telling us how or why.
- **Qualitative research:** Rather than focusing on numbers, this type of research 'uses broader questions and themes and patterns' (Parsons, 2020, 4). This data is better at answering the 'how' and 'why' questions.
- **Segmentation:** Segmentation seeks to understand visitor behaviour by categorising people into groups based on similar characteristics.
- **Front-end evaluation:** This is research carried out before a project to inform planning.
- **Formative evaluation:** 'is conducted before the project is completely finalised – i.e. do some research a few months into the project with audiences to see if you are still on track' (MGS, 2022).
- **Remedial evaluation:** Remedial evaluation happens when much of the work has been done, but there are still opportunities to make changes if needed. As Kate Haley Goldman, writing for Dexibit, says: 'Remedial evaluation occurs in that sweet spot during a soft launch . . . we're working the last kinks out' (Haley Goldman, 2022). If you are undertaking regular visitor experience measuring (i.e., not project-based), it will most likely come under remedial evaluation.
- **Summative evaluation:** This happens at the end of a project to assess whether or not the goals have been achieved.

There are two important takeaways from the wider world of museum evaluation that are useful for measuring the visitor experience.

The first is that among all the different types of evaluation there is no silver bullet. Maya Sharma, writing for The Audience Agency, says 'there is no single 'right' tool' (Sharma, 2022), whilst Emma Parsons, writing the audience research guide for AIM, says that different approaches need to be combined to achieve 'real insight' (Parsons, 2020, 4). That's why, when we look at the different ways of measuring visitor experience later in this chapter, I'll strongly encourage you to mix and match methods, depending on the goals of your organisation.

Secondly, all evaluators agree that good evaluation should be a cycle, not a straight line. Emma Parsons' diagram (Figure 12.1 opposite) shows that evaluation is an ongoing process. There's no point in measuring your visitor experience once and then resting on your laurels for the rest of the year. Things change. And, as Parsons comments: 'Gathering data to better understand audiences often throws up yet more questions that you want to find answers to' (Parsons, 2020, 14).

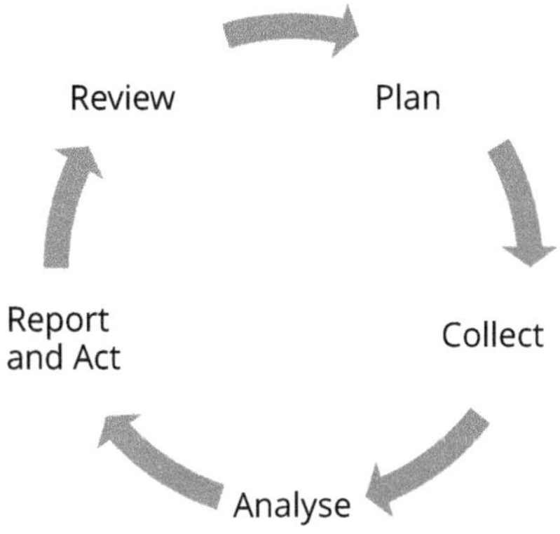

Figure 12.1 *Evaluation cycle.* Source: Emma Parsons, 2020

What are we measuring?

The first step to measuring your visitor experience is understanding exactly what you want to find out. Many museums and sector bodies look to assess the satisfaction of visitors, but even that is a nebulous concept. What is satisfaction? Is it the same for everyone?

John Falk suggests that in a cultural experience, satisfaction depends on the gap between the expectations of a visitor and the actual experience they have (Falk, 2009, 117). This will ring true to many Visitor Experience professionals but it does mean that, as a concept, it varies across different people. Nevertheless, 'satisfaction' has come to be recognised as a common way to measure visitor experiences, because it is a reliable indicator of whether people will visit again, and whether they will recommend the experience to others (Falk, 2009, 118). In evaluation terms, this is often referred to as a 'net promoter' score or NPS.

The other problem with knowing what to measure comes with the perennial problem of defining just what exactly we mean by 'the visitor experience'. My belief that the visitor experience should be a holistic understanding of how a visitor engages with every aspect of the museum has been explored in previous chapters, so I think it only remains to say (perhaps predictably) that I believe we should also take a holistic approach to experience evaluation. This means including all elements of the experience in the visitor journey, including the lifts, the toilets and even other visitors. No one part of the visitor experience is more important than the other, and none can be measured in isolation. Sometimes efficiency drives us to measure only what we can directly control; but doing so denies us a full understanding of the experience of our visitors.

Falk also points out that, historically, there has been a lack of accurate and valid evaluation tools with which to measure the visitor experience (Falk, 2009, 248). This area, however, has evolved in the last 20 years and practitioners are now faced with a veritable menu of evaluation methods to choose from.

Methods of evaluation

Questionnaires

Questionnaires are probably amongst the most common type of evaluation tool used in museums. You've probably filled one in yourself, but beware! We are naturally drawn to fill in museum questionnaires because we work in the sector and are interested in how our friends and neighbours are doing things. Most visitors are not museum people and therefore self-completion questionnaires (like the type you might e-mail a visitor after a visit) have a notoriously low take-up. Even when they are completed, they might not necessarily give a representative picture. The Renaissance East of England Evaluation Toolkit offers advice on this topic, warning that 'it tends to be highly motivated people who do participate, often having had polarised experiences' (Renaissance East of England, 2008, 31). You'll get a more representative sample by using the survey to interview people on site, but obviously this comes with a need for staffing resource.

Questionnaires are great for capturing demographic data and easily quantifiable information, such as where someone first heard about the museum. Although they are most commonly used for gathering quantitative data, nuanced information can be gained through questionnaires by including a mix of question styles. For example, you can ask attitudinal questions using a Likert scale of five or six points, like the example in Figure 12.2. Typically, though, if you want really in-depth information about your visitors' opinions and attitudes, you might choose a richer evaluation method more focused on qualitative data, such as accompanied visits.

How do you feel about the level of customer service you received today?

Fell below expectations					Exceeded expectations
1	2	3	4	5	6

Figure 12.2 *Example of a Likert scale question*

Accompanied visits

The accompanied visit (in other words, a museum employee or researcher walking around with a visitor as they experience the museum) is an evaluation method that not only offers a good insight into how your visitors engage with the museum and what they get from the visit, but often how previous experiences and backgrounds can influence visit expectations.

There are various ways of undertaking an accompanied visit. You can recruit participants ahead of time and meet them on site. You can meet up with them beforehand to understand prior experience. You can even 'accompany' visitors by stealth, using tracking or video equipment to do so without affecting the visit. Researchers can actively engage the visitors in conversation about what they are seeing or doing, or they can remain silent; observing interactions in the visitor group and documenting conversations. Participants can also be asked to complete tasks, such as make a video or keep a diary.

In her 2018 article reflecting on different types of accompanied visits in attractions, researcher Naomi Haywood explains that the approach chosen for the visit should depend on the research goals of the institution. She coins a new typology spectrum for visits, from 'thick' visits, where the researcher spends a lot of time with the participant before and after, and gains a rich level of detail about their experience, at one end; to 'thin' visits, which might consist of an observation followed by some brief questions. No one approach is better or worse than another; it just depends on the information you need to obtain, as well as other factors such as sample size, timeframe, cost and logistics (Haywood, 2018, 144).

All accompanied visits have one key advantage over surveys and questionnaires. As Haywood puts it: 'Accompanied visits provide information about what visitors actually do in museums, as opposed to only what they say they do' (Haywood, 2018, 137).

Traditional feedback

By traditional feedback, I don't necessarily mean snail mail. It could be e-mails, phone calls or letters, but the one common factor is lack of solicitation. These visitors haven't been asked, but they want to tell us something, and it's ended up with your contact centre or in your generic museum e-mail inbox.

Unsolicited feedback is generally driven by extreme attitudes. People are unlikely to get in touch with you this way to tell you they had an okay visit; it was either terrible or it was the best day of their life. Does this mean it isn't reflective of the visitor experience? Not necessarily: it's still important to monitor trends and its useful to have insight into these individual snapshots. Just be aware that you may not be seeing the whole picture.

Traditional feedback has, of course, decreased substantially over the last 20 years thanks to a plethora of other channels which visitors have to make their views known. However, some audiences, particularly elderly people, still favour these traditional channels. Therefore, if this group makes up a large portion of your audience, you should make sure that you are still investing some resource into managing this area. You can make this easier by setting up policies to govern how your organisation responds, such as automatic acknowledgements and pre-defined timeframes to resolve issues. Remember, service recovery is still part of that engagement with visitors, so even though you are measuring the visitor experience, be aware that you're actually still in the process of delivering it, and therefore still have a chance to shape your visitors' perceptions.

Social media reviews

One of the biggest areas for measuring the visitor experience today is on social media. Trip Advisor alone contained more than 860 million reviews at the time of writing, and that's far from the only option (Trip Advisor, 2021b). Facebook also offers a review service, as do Google and many other platforms. There are, of course, far too many to review, so it's important to choose wisely. Some agencies provide platforms where you can review all mentions of your museum, and aggregate all reviews from all over the internet but, of course, there is a cost associated with this. If you don't have this resource, I would suggest doing an initial deep dive into as many different sites as possible to get as much information as you can, and then commit to reviewing a couple of channels every month based on which platforms are most popular with your audience.

Social media comments and reviews are generally much more realistic than traditional feedback because they are less likely to be motivated by extremes. However, be aware that social media absolutely can be affected by trends and news stories, so sometimes you might see odd spikes that aren't actually about your visitor experience at all.

Anecdotal feedback

Anecdotal feedback is one of the most important measures of the visitor experience, and I've deliberately put it right in the middle of this list because so often it's an afterthought. Not only is asking your front-facing staff about anecdotal feedback a mark of respect for their experience and expertise, it's the easiest, cheapest and most direct way of finding out how your visitors are feeling.

Detractors might tell you that you'll never hear bad feedback about front-facing staff from front-facing staff; and of course, there is probably an element of truth there. But in my opinion the advantages far outweigh this point. Visitors say things to staff (or to each other, near staff) that they wouldn't bother writing in about, or putting on Trip Advisor. And often it's those middling opinions that really help to build the full picture. Also, nothing matches the immediacy of anecdotal feedback. This can be of particular importance when trialling something new, because then the operation can be adapted or tweaked straightaway, based on what visitors are saying.

So how do you measure anecdotal feedback? I've tried a few different ways in the past, including keeping a book in the tea room for staff to note down comments as they hear them, then reviewing the comments and coding them as positive or negative, or asking front-facing team reps to gather feedback at regular meetings. I've probably yet to hit on the perfect method but, still, it's important that this measurement is included and valued in the same way as more formal feedback channels.

My colleague Emma Morioka, Customer Insight Manager at Historic Royal Palaces, agrees with the importance of anecdotal feedback: 'It is invaluable. I have found that the more structured it is, the better. Develop two or three key questions and then ask staff to answer them either as a one-off exercise or on a regular basis. Questions could be things like: What works for visitors? What doesn't work? How could we make it better?' (interview with author, 2021).

Visitor books and comment cards

On-site methods of small-scale feedback collection come in various guises. If your comment card has different questions and options on it, it's probably a self-complete survey or questionnaire rather than a comment card. Blank comment cards, whether they remain on display or go in a box, are more similar to visitor books, in that you have no control over what visitors write. This can be really valuable, because the lack of direction means visitors have the freedom to put their impressions into their own words. Other times, visitor book contributions can be less useful, such as the classic swear words or even, in one notable example at Kew Palace, the full lyrics to 'I'll be Back' from *Hamilton: an American musical.*

On any platform where people can read other people's comments before contributing, such as open visitor books, there can also be an issue of bias. People may read other people's comments and build upon them rather than forming their own opinions. For comments and details that remain on display, there are all sorts of issues, from paper waste to having the resource to police obscenities to data protection (for some reason, some visitors still insist on writing out their full postal address in an open visitor book). So, whilst these channels can provide some useful insights into the visitor experience, sometimes they can be more trouble than they are worth!

Mystery visitors

Mystery visitors are a great way of getting very rich, detailed information about the visitor experience. Although they only give a snapshot of one particular experience on one particular day, the level of detail obtainable is unparalleled – when it's done right.

For me, it all comes down to the brief. When commissioning a mystery visit company, you need to be very clear on what exactly you want the visitors to do and measure. Using your visitor journey framework to help inform this is a good way of making sure the standards you want checked are the right ones. Also, make sure that when things change, you remember to update the questionnaire for the company, so that what you are measuring is always relevant and you're not paying for out-of-date information. If you can keep on top of this information flow, you should see some really valuable results.

For many, the cost of a mystery shopper is the real barrier to this method. However, there are ways around this. Many museum groups and networks have set up reciprocal mystery visit schemes, where staff visit each other's sites and provide feedback. Museum staff, of course, will never be able to provide the objective view of an external visitor, but as long as this is taken into account and understood when reviewing the data, this can be a good, cost-effective method of accessing this channel.

One important caveat with this method is to let your team know a mystery visit is happening. They may not know the exact day (you may not either) but they should know beforehand that they are going to be measured in this way and how the feedback will be actioned.

Measuring feelings

I'm including one final method here borrowed from my friend and well-known museum anarchist Franklin Vagnone, because I think it's a really interesting approach to gathering a feelings-over-facts impression of the visitor experience. In working groups across several historic houses, Vagnone has used what he and Deborah Ryan call an Imagination, Excitement and Energy or IEE Graph (Vagnone and Ryan, 2016, 210). In an IEE Graph, visitors to a historic house are asked to track their levels of imagination, energy and excitement through the use of broad prompts. The finished product shows a kind of stream of consciousness, demonstrating how emotions and feelings can be influenced by situational factors ('it's super-hot in this room') and content ('they were obviously a wealthy family') (Vagnone and Ryan, 2016, 212).

This approach might not work for your particular site, but it's worth giving some thought to how emotions and feelings can be measured, since we know they are such a huge part of the visitor experience.

Analysis

Analysing the data you end up with is as important a part of the evaluation process as collecting it and taking action. It's critical to set aside the resource to do this properly at the start of the undertaking. As MGS advise: 'Consider what you want to know and how you will analyse it at the project's outset, making sure you have the time required' (MGS, 2022).

How you analyse data will depend on the type of data you have collected. For quantitative data, you will need to consider how to categorise the information. Then, you can cross-tabulate to give you more information and insight. For example, how many of your repeat visitors live nearby? MGS advise that low numbers in quantitative studies should be treated carefully: 'If more than 50 people have been included in the study use percentages. If less than 50 then state "number of respondents". If you use percentages for a small sample, it can be misleading' (MGS, 2022).

When it comes to qualitative data, you will need to be less numbers-driven when it comes to analysis and instead look for themes, patterns. Parsons advises 'looking at issues such as what people engage with and what prevents them from doing so' (Parsons, 2020). Obviously, the types of questions you will be asking depends on your research goals, but it's important to keep an open mind when analysing qualitative data. When it comes to arranging for presentation, use quotes to illustrate specific view points, but remember not to attribute them to actual named people.

Choosing the right mix of methods

As mentioned earlier, no single evaluation method is perfect, and they all have their advantages and disadvantages. For that reason, I would advocate using a mix of methods, so that together, they can provide as accurate a picture as possible.

There are two basic scenarios where you might be looking to measure the visitor experience; it could be a one-off deep dive to inform long-term planning, the development of a Visitor Experience Strategy or a capital project. For this scenario, I would suggest collecting as much data as you can, not just about the current experience, but about how all stakeholders, including visitors, non-visitors and front-facing staff see the experience developing in the future.

More common though, is the need for continuous measurement: our month-on-month view of how we are performing. This approach is a harder balance to strike; it has to be comprehensive enough to give us actionable data, but light-touch enough to be achievable each month. If you have the budget to outsource the number crunching, that makes things a lot easier. However, many museums don't, and therefore you might need to think about how to make this exercise realistic within existing resource.

One option is a syndicated service, as Emma Morioka highlights:

> . . . there are a number of syndicated services available where museums and attractions pool resources together and a research agency designs and runs the survey and data processing/analysis on behalf of each subscriber . . . this is how a lot of museums, galleries and attractions do their continuous visitor satisfaction and profiling surveys.

Taking action

When you finally have that coveted holistic understanding of the visitor experience, the most important question is what you do with it. The biggest mistake would be to spend time and money gleaning all this data and then leave it sitting in an unread report on a drive or folder somewhere. So, what action should you take?

In the past, I have found it useful to convene a specific, cross-museum group to look at the holistic visitor experience and so, for me, that was the perfect forum to present this information. The cross-museum nature of it was important. Although as operators we 'own' the visitor experience, hence the reason it often falls to us to do the evaluative legwork, it's important to underline the fact that delivery of the visitor experience is a shared responsibility for all museum staff. This is particularly important in large museums, where departments are more likely to be siloed or even outsourced, but it's also important for smaller museums to make sure everyone is on the same page.

Having a specific, regular forum to look at all of this stuff means that it doesn't drop off the radar after a few months and that everyone has a way of noting actions and reporting back on them at a later date. Actions can be simple, such as increasing amounts of a popular and often sold-out food item in the café, but they can often be more complex than that. For example, if the complaint is a visitor being given the wrong information by a member of staff, the action might be 'staff to give visitors correct information' but actually it's more likely to be 'review staff training', or even more likely to be 'review communication channels between departments'. Often, when the same customer service issues recur month after month, it's because there is a deeper organisational reason for issues on the floor, so make sure your actions are aimed at the root of the problem and not just the symptoms.

It's not just about problems. One of the most important things you can do with this information is celebrate success. Not only does it put everyone in a great mood to have their achievements recognised, it clearly articulates what excellent performance looks like, and can be held up as a shining example. Where possible, if individual staff can be identified, make sure they are recognised. An internal customer service award is a great idea, and something I have introduced to many teams. You don't need to have a huge budget for prizes and awards; the most important thing is that teams delivering customer service can see that good performance is recognised and valued within the organisation.

Case Study 12: Measuring customer service at the Natural History Museum

The process of assessing evaluation needs described above, picking the right methods and then taking action, is exactly the thought process I went through when I was asked to develop and deliver a new Customer Service Strategy at the Natural History Museum (NHM) in London.

I should say that this work happened in 2015; 'customer service' is not a phrase I particularly like to use anymore. Not only does the word 'customer' sound incredibly commercial (which isn't always our main goal in museums), 'service' itself speaks of something brief, one-way and transactional. 'Customer service' makes me think of those old corporate training videos where staff are instructed to smile, or say please and thank you. Nowadays, I prefer the phrase 'visitor engagement', which to me is much more interactive and all-encompassing.

However, back in 2015, my thinking hadn't progressed that far. In fact, I'd never attempted this kind of project at an organisational level before. So, my first step was to get a really good, detailed picture of where we were in terms of customer service, and comparing that to our desired future. My team ran workshops across all different Museum teams gathering feedback on what the current barriers were and suggestions for improvement. We also mined every available channel we could for visitor feedback.

However, even a national museum like the NHM wouldn't have been able to commit the resources to monitoring customer service in such a detailed and in-depth way on a continual basis. We needed to find a manageable balance. We did have some external support, with a mystery visit and social media monitoring agency helping out, but much of the monitoring and compiling was done in-house. This couldn't have been achieved without putting in that early work with the workshops; all departments needed to feel involved and invested in order to contribute resource in this way.

I selected a mix of four channels within my department (although I should add that Marketing teams also did annual visitor surveys). Those channels were traditional feedback, social media comments, a Mystery Visit scheme, and anecdotal feedback from the floor. I felt that gave me a good mix of opinion – from the extreme to the banal – and a nice variety of detail: from the swathes of online one-line reviewers to the intense specifics of a Mystery Visitor. Together, they showed me a good all-round picture of how we were performing that month.

As I advised earlier, I then created a cross-museum forum focused on customer service. We called it the Customer Service Insight Group, or CSIG. The group included operational managers from all the front-facing departments, even those of outsourced functions. We were responsible for shepherding and progressing some of the objectives in the wider new Customer Service Strategy, as well as gathering, monitoring and actioning the results from our four selected channels.

A really important role for the group was in recognising success. Not only did I publish the results of each month across the Museum intranet, but CSIG also came together as a judging panel for an internal customer service award. This award has now been running for several years, with the first two annual winners coming from the Security and Catering teams. This was particularly cheering, not only as it's an example of how teams commonly outsourced can be made to feel more engaged with the organisation, but because I feel they are two departments that are not celebrated often enough in the wider cultural sector.

Each museum has different needs and will choose to measure the visitor experience differently. However, for me, the three key ideas that every museum should take on board are: make your measurements as holistic as possible; listen to what your front-facing teams are telling you and, finally, celebrate success.

CHAPTER 13

Creating a Visitor Experience Strategy

> Make your plan like bamboo… flexible to bend but not break in the wind.
>
> (Brilliant Idea Studio)

This section of the book is all about setting the vision and taking responsibility for developing the visitor experience at your organisation. However, this doesn't mean it's something you can do alone. Museums are always a collaboration. Different parties hold a stake in that vision, including staff, volunteers, trustees, audiences who visit all the time and audiences who haven't yet set foot in your museum. So, when it comes to developing the visitor experience, it's important to bring in different voices all the way through.

A really useful way of doing this is to develop and deliver a plan that sets out the organisational approach to Visitor Experience, brings in feedback and other views to articulate the current reality and sets the future direction.

Developing a plan like this helps you:

- bring in different voices and opinions
- develop a clear picture of where you are and where you want to go
- agree on what success looks like and how you will measure it
- plan and commit the resources you need to get there
- get buy-in from different stakeholders within the museum
- demonstrate the value of the visitor experience to the organisation and other stakeholders
- demonstrate how delivering on your visitor experience objectives can help realise the wider organisational vision.

Some museums will call this plan a 'Visitor Experience Strategy'. It might be a lengthy stand-alone document, or for others it may be a smaller part of an overall business plan. Some museums have a whole suite of 'strategy' documents, some won't have any. It really doesn't matter what format your

Visitor Experience Strategy takes. Although in this chapter we'll look at some examples of how different museums and heritage organisations have articulated their strategies, what I'm really hoping to do is inspire you to have a deep think about where your visitor experience is going, and give you some tools to bring others along on the journey.

What is a Visitor Experience Strategy?

A good definition of a Visitor Experience Strategy comes from the introduction of the National Museum of Wales's own Strategy:

> This document outlines our ambitions for Visitor Experience between 2018 and 2021. It defines our responsibilities to our visitors, through a Customer Service Charter. It provides guidelines for upholding these responsibilities, through specific Aims and Objectives. This strategy outlines how we will maintain and share good practice, how we will improve visitors' experiences by making specific changes, and how we will measure our success.
>
> (AC – NMW, 2018, 3)

However, even if your organisation doesn't have Aims, Objectives or Charters, it doesn't mean you can't have a blueprint for developing the visitor experience.

Cultural consultancy Brilliant Idea Studio (2022) defines a Visitor Experience Strategy as 'an encompassing plan that signals to the whole organisation how patrons should experience your space. This plan should serve as a foundation for any part of your organisation that touches your visitor (likely all of it).' It's also a plan for action: 'A strategy is a way of saying that you are creating a plan of action, a road map, and some rules when something confounds your plan or map.' So, although formats and styles can vary, if you do want to develop your own Visitor Experience Strategy, I would suggest spending some time thinking about four key areas:

1 research and development
2 one big idea
3 getting buy-in
4 SMART goals.

Research and development

Before thinking about what your museum's visitor experience will look like in the future, get a clear idea of where it is now. You can get lots of ideas and information about how to do this in the previous chapter of this book, 'Measuring the Visitor Experience'. Examples from other museum Visitor Experience Strategies show how research can be used to inform a plan. For example, English Heritage's Visitor Experience Strategy references the results of market research and visitor surveys. The Visitor Experience Strategy of the National Museum Wales begins:

> This document draws from extensive research, evaluation, consultation and benchmarking. Staff at all seven museums and the Collections Centre have given their feedback – as well as the visiting public, non-visitors and critical friends from the museums sector and beyond.
>
> (AC – NMW, 2018, 3)

Utilising these varied sources of data helps museums avoid making the mistake of ignoring primary visitor needs, as the Strategy goes on to state: 'These survey responses point to a need to implement a 'back to basics' approach to improving Visitor Experience ensuring our sites are accessible, easily navigable, comfortable and engaging' (AC – NMW, 2018, 14). It's easy to get lost in the high aspirational aims of a strategy, but focusing on visitor feedback will help you include (and therefore get sign-off on) the basic things that need to be fixed as well.

It's also important to carry out research and development when it comes to defining your future vision. In *Anarchist's Guide to Historic House Museum*, Franklin Vagnone and Deborah Ryan talk about community research being the key to defining your strategy and purpose:

> Stop expecting people to be interested in what you have been offering. Be willing to re-think the types and methodologies that shape your visitor's experience and ensure that it is both socially relevant to your surrounding neighbourhood and personally compelling. In addressing a cultural disconnect, provide opportunities to build community by doing good. Make sure that understanding your community is a top priority.
>
> (Vagnone and Ryan, 2016, 50)

Vagnone and Ryan go on to advise that 'becoming familiar with your neighbours is the first step. Research that focuses on learning about them should be undertaken with the same enthusiasm that has gone into learning about your museum and the artefacts it houses' (p. 51).

Look internally as well. Other departments in the museum might be working on their own strategies, and none should be done in isolation. For example, a Learning Strategy might inform your thinking when it comes to access and inclusion within your Visitor Experience Strategy. Additionally, other teams, for example Marketing or Interpretation teams, may have already done research about your audiences.

One big idea

When developing a Visitor Experience Strategy, I find it useful (and also motivational) to have one big idea to shape your plan around. This can add focus to your vision, help you galvanise your stakeholders around your strategy and help you prioritise your objectives. Your 'one big idea' should meet the needs identified in your research and development and it should link to the wider vision of the organisation.

In reading Visitor Experience Strategies from other museums (many are available online), I can see lots of evidence of the strength of the 'one big idea' approach. English Heritage (EH), for example, explicitly state their 'one big idea' as 'Visitors First'. 'We'll put our visitors at the heart of our work', they state in their current strategy, 'from planning to delivery' (EH, 2019, 2).

When I was involved in developing the Visitor Experience Strategy at the Natural History Museum (NHM), we had a similar idea: looking at the experience holistically, from a visitor point of view. This may seem like an obvious idea for Visitor Experience Strategies to be built on, but actually it created impactful change. It meant we no longer excused poor service because that part of the operation was contracted out, or because it came from a different department. Looking at things from the visitor's point of view meant that we had to care about every aspect of the experience; even the parts we didn't have direct control over. That had real consequences for how the visitor experience was managed, and was a step change in our approach at the time. So, even little objectives, such as ensuring contractors had access to NHM communications channels and training, came from that one, original, big idea.

Whilst a Visitor Experience Strategy can encompass many future goals, sometimes one big idea can be the driving force behind everything a museum does. You'll read about how powerful and impactful one big idea can be in the case study at the end of this chapter.

Getting buy-in

Whilst front-facing VE teams will be the primary movers and deliverers of your strategy, it's important to acknowledge that the visitor experience touches every museum employee: it's everyone's responsibility. That holistic vision was the key piece of the NHM Strategy, and shows up in others too.

For example, in the National Museum Wales (AC – NWM) Visitor Experience Strategy:

> This is a document for all our staff. Even though some of us don't interact with our visitors on a daily basis, the decisions we make and the way we work has an impact on our visitors' experiences at our museums.
>
> (AC – NMW, 2018, 3)

A good way to get buy-in from all staff for your strategy is to make it very clear that the visitor experience objectives link directly to the overall organisational vision. For example, the English Heritage Visitor Experience Strategy (Figure 13.1) is explicit in stating that its purpose is to support the wider organisation: 'The English Heritage Strategy has four key pillars. The Visitor Experience Strategy has been designed to support each of these' (EH, 2019, 4). The English Heritage Visitor Experience Team are in the process of formulating the next iteration of their strategy to strengthen the key pillars, underpinned by a renewed focus on its people and on equity, diversity and inclusion.

INSPIRATION
We will:

- Improve the ways we bring history to life, for every visitor, every day
- Improve brand warmth
- Focus on storytelling to deliver fun, authentic experiences
- Develop new volunteer programmes
- Enhance our 'everyday' offer and add value to membership
- Become even more family friendly

INVOLVEMENT
We'll win more support by:

- Creating exciting new opportunities for volunteers to bring history to life
- Engaging with local communities
- Improving our training for site teams
- Empowering site teams to deliver fun experiences through storytelling
- Improving education facilities
- Becoming more accessible and welcoming to diverse audiences

FINANCIAL SUSTAINABILITY
Our improved Visitor Experience will:

- Increase visitor numbers
- Increase dwell time and secondary spend
- Increase repeat visitation
- Strengthen our offer to Members

CONSERVATION & STEWARDSHIP
We'll support Conservation & Stewardship by:

- Running Conservation in Action programmes
- Creating play experiences for families inspired by our conservation work

Figure 13.1 *English Heritage Visitor Experience Strategy 2023.* Source: English Heritage (2019)

At Historic Royal Palaces (HRP), we have an organisational goal to increase access to our Palaces and for them to be places where everyone can come: to 'create space to stir and be stirred' (HRP, 2022). Our visual representation of that brand idea, in our posters and logo, utilises a reference to the *enfilade*, a suite of adjoining rooms in a palace (see Figure 13.2). This suite would get you closer and closer to the presence of the monarch, and symbolises our wish to bring our visitors closer to the heart of the action.

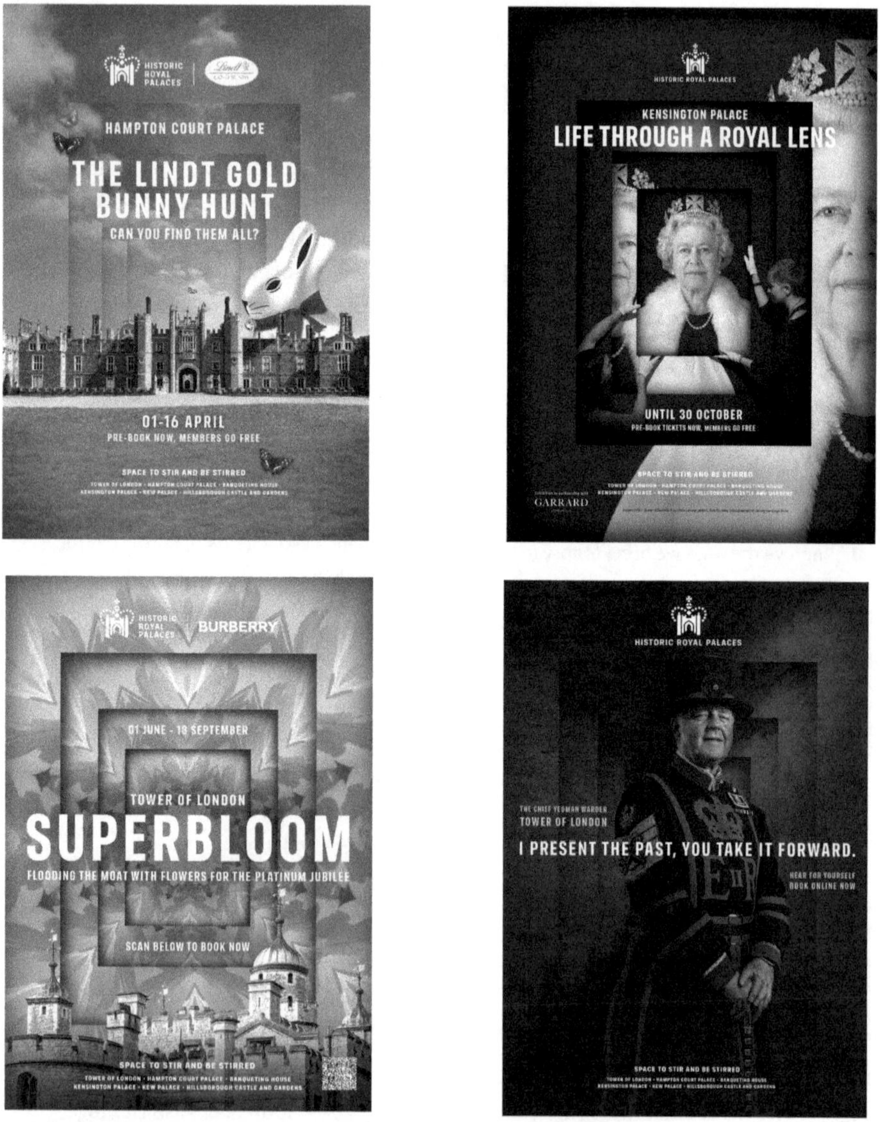

Figure 13.2 *Examples of HRP visual identity.* Source: Historic Royal Palaces (2022)

We don't actually have an official Visitor Experience Strategy at HRP. Our version is called the 'Royal Standard' and it's our description of how we deliver face-to-face visitor engagement. In it, we talk about how our approach to the visitor experience mirrors our brand, and is informed by the aim of bringing our visitors closer to us by being more inclusive, removing barriers and reaching wider audiences. By expressing our goals this way, we make the link between Visitor Experience and our brand very clear, and this helps everyone get on board, even if they don't specifically work in Visitor Experience teams.

Some museums have chosen to tie their overall strategies and Visitor Experience Strategies together in one strategy or business plan. The advantage of this approach is that it links the Visitor Experience objectives very clearly to organisational goals. For example, the Business Plan for the Thackray Museum of Medicine states:

> Through Consolidation, Impact and Sustainability we will share our strength and solidarity with our communities to deliver, together, a museum that is ambitious, dynamic and inclusive
>
> (Thackray Museum, 2022, 3)

Then, later in the document, objectives for the Consolidation strand are listed, including:

> We will . . .
>
> - Create a better-defined development path for our Team
> - Build on excellence to raise even higher the quality of our visitor experience
>
> (Thackray Museum, 2022, 10)

The objectives for Visitor Experience are therefore understood in the light of the wider consolidation work the museum is doing to build on its success.

As well as colleagues in other departments, a Visitor Experience Strategy is also the starting point for getting your delivery teams on board with the future vision. It's really important to get the front-facing teams on the same page; after all, they will be the ones delivering your vision on the floor.

To do this, it needs to be clear that the Strategy is delivering things they want to see. Their thoughts and input should have been gathered as part of the research and development; they hear what visitors say and see what they do more than anyone else on the museum staff. Take care to address these issues explicitly in the objectives of your strategy. Finding a couple of quick wins can really help build the momentum and energy needed to deliver the longer-term goals.

Make sure you have considered development for your delivery teams as part of your Strategy. For example, the English Heritage Visitor Experience Strategy states:

> Our site staff and volunteers are a major asset. Their customer service consistently scores highly in visitor surveys and mystery shopper exercises. They often have a real passion for history and for sharing the histories of their sites, and we want to harness that passion . . . Site staff will be empowered to adapt to their audiences, rather than stick rigidly to scripts . . . We will create new tours about stories of our sites that have been under represented in the past. This includes the stories of people from diverse backgrounds.
>
> (EH, 2019, 14)

Here, the EH Visitor Experience Strategy is setting a vision for Visitor Experience staff development that is then fleshed out with objectives and further planning. Similarly, your Visitor Experience Strategy may well be the starting point for a new training plan. We'll talk more about training plans in the next chapter.

SMART goals

If you really want to get buy-in for your strategy and use it to raise the profile of Visitor Experience, you have to be able to show that you are delivering against its goals. To do this effectively, your objectives should be SMART: Specific, Measurable, Attributable, Realistic and Timely (Doran, 1981).

Take the time to think about how your objectives will be measured. Will you see an increase in mystery shopper scores? Will you benchmark against other organisations? Will you retain staff for longer? Will your Gift Aid conversion go up? If so, by how much? How regularly will you pause to measure progress and through what forums? Define these targets and then use them as your key performance indicators going forward.

The Thackray Museum of Medicine Business Plan shows us a good example of how this works in practice. Here, an action plan takes a strategic objective, for example: 'Measuring Performance: carry out a programme of quality improvements to visitor operations' and assigns a lead team (in this case, Operations) and a target/measure: 'Increased VAQAS (Visitor Attraction Quality Assurance Service) score on 2021 rating (905). Increased Net Promoter Score from public evaluation and qualitative visitor feedback' (Thackray Museum, 2022, 13).

By backing up your goals with measurable targets, you'll be able to demonstrate the value Visitor Experience is delivering for the organisation as a whole, as well as show just how effective and high-performing your team is!

There are some circumstances however, when things don't go to plan. It's worth thinking about this as well. Some museum Visitor Experience Strategies will have a risk register attached that plots the possible things that could go wrong and the impact they would have on delivering the strategy. Whilst this is a useful approach, it's also important to think about the things you can't foresee. That's why the Brilliant Idea Studio advise: 'Make your plan like bamboo . . . flexible to bend but not break in the wind. Keep that image in your mind as you create a plan. Your plan should be able to take some challenges but not break' (Brilliant Idea Studio, 2022). Despite this uncertainty, having a risk register will help your organisation or team be more resilient, as you will be familiar with how to work through problems and apply mitigations. Table 13.1 is an example.

Table 13.1 *Risk register example*

No.	Risk	Description	Impact	Probability	Score	Mitigation
1	Short-staffing	Unable to deliver public programme due to illness	1	3	3	Work out hierarchy of programme. Train reserves.
2	Adverse weather	Unable to open due to bad weather	4	1	4	Create adverse weather policy. Indoor back-up spaces identified.

Case Study 13: The London Museum of Water and Steam

In my work, I've come across a few arguments against creating a Visitor Experience Strategy. One is that they can be meaningless. If a Visitor Experience Strategy is written, put on a shelf and never looked at again, it certainly will be meaningless. However, that choice is very much up to you. If you put in the work to make your Visitor Experience Strategy a dynamic, living, guiding document then it can be.

Another common argument is time and resource. If you work in a small museum where there aren't different departments and everyone mucks in together, you might not feel the need to create a plan or a strategy about how you want to develop Visitor Experience. However, as this chapter has shown, this work can be combined with other documents, such as your business plan. The format and location of your Visitor Experience Strategy really doesn't matter. It's the thought, the work and the vision that are important.

The case study here demonstrates this latter point perfectly. The London Museum of Water and Steam is a small, independent museum in Brentford, west London. Their little team doesn't have the time and resource to pump out endless strategies, but they do have 'one big idea' that has shaped their approach to how they deliver the visitor experience.

Recently, Museum trustees redeveloped the Museum's business plan, to suit the role that Museum Director Liz Power felt the Museum should play in the local community. 'Our community programming really stated to develop in 2019' says Power. 'It has always been led by the needs of the local community and focused on sharing our spaces with them' (Power, 2021).

This idea was already in place by the beginning of 2020. Then, when the pandemic hit, this strategy shaped the Museum response. 'When the Museum was closed, and the staff team was furloughed in March 2020, we needed to decide what was the right next step for the Museum' says Power. 'The trustees applied for support from Arts Council England. But instead of applying for support to reopen the Museum in Summer 2020 we instead decided to create a new outdoor offer for our local community. The Museum is surrounded by flats, both social and private accommodation. We thought about what the families in those flats would need the most that summer, and the thought that they had been up in their flats looking down at our site stuck in our mind. We transformed our car park with children's scooters, opened our water play for free, and put activities in our garden. For three months the local community played in the spaces, with many families visiting the site for the first time. We gave our regular summer visitors "golden tickets" to be the first visitors back in the Museum when we reopened.'

'Each time we have reopened, before the public have come in, we have held a week of events for local community groups, showing people the Museum, talking to them about what they would like from us whilst building partnerships', continues Power. This strategy has helped ensure buy-in from the local community, who, Power says 'are more at the centre of our future planning than ever. The support from our local families was seen in the summer of 2021 when the local community returned in larger numbers than ever expected to the Museum.'

This small, independent museum then, without developing a lengthy Visitor Experience Strategy document, has done its research and development, come up with 'one big idea' or guiding principle based on that research, has ensured buy-in with the local community by engaging with them and giving them what they need, and through all of this, has achieved the objectives set in its business plan and achieved a sustainable future. This work, Power says, 'will enable us to fulfil our aim as an organisation, by being loved by our community, volunteers and stakeholder.'

CHAPTER 14

Continuing Development and Engagement

> We spend too long in the sector building our own versions of the same approach for front of house teams, when we could get a lot further, a lot faster by sharing opportunities across our teams and organisations.
>
> (David Hingley, Tate)

In the first part of this book, we spoke about how to deliver a great induction for new staff. However, engagement and development of your team should not be something that only happens in their first week. It's important to keep staff engaged throughout their time at your organisation and especially if you are looking to evolve and improve the visitor experience.

The desire to keep training going throughout the employee journey is always up against the challenges of the museum environment. The main one is time, both in developing and delivering from a management point of view and often the sheer impossibility of getting frontline staff away from the floor long enough to be able to train them. Scarcity of time can also lead to lack of strategic planning, with training becoming sporadic or piecemeal as a result.

When thinking about what kind of training visitor-facing staff need, we are also grappling with the constant, ever-evolving conversation about what visitor engagement is, what the Visitor Experience role is expected to deliver and what skills need to be developed in order to meet our goals in this area.

Finally, as staff move from being new recruits to established employees, it can be hard to identify genuine and fruitful continuing development opportunities, especially when dealing with large, diverse teams, and therefore, a variety of learning styles and goals.

This chapter will touch on all of these challenges, and hopefully suggest some ways you can meet them.

Employee engagement

Before we talk about training and development, it's important to say that these are not the only tools of employee engagement. When something goes wrong in the Visitor Experience teams, its common to blame lack of training, but just as important as formal development is the culture of engagement in the organisation.

Back in 2009, David MacLeod and Nita Clarke prepared a report for the UK Government, *Engage for Success*, which proved high performance within organisations is linked directly to employee engagement (MacLeod and Clarke, 2009a). Through analysis of hundreds of case studies across many sectors, they identified four enablers of engagement: values shared by organisations with high levels of employee engagement (see Table 14.1). In the museum setting, these values can positively transform the staff, and ultimately, the visitor experience.

Table 14.1 *Engage for Success: the four enablers.* Source: MacLeod and Clarke, 2009b

Enabler	Definition
Strategic narrative	Visible, empowering leadership providing a strong strategic narrative about the organisation, where it's come from and where it's going.
Engaging managers	Engaging managers who focus their people and give them scope, treat their people as individuals and coach and stretch their people.
Employee voice	Employee voice throughout the organisation, for reinforcing and challenging views, between functions and externally. Employees are seen not as the problem, rather as central to the solution, to be involved, listened to, and invited to contribute their experience, expertise and ideas.
Organisational integrity	The values on the wall are reflected in day-to-day behaviours. There is a gap between what is said and what is done. Promises made and promises kept, or an explanation given as to why not.

As MacLeod and Clarke state, the enablers are not a 'how-to' guide. 'However,' they write, 'we were struck in the course of the review how often the same four broad enablers/drivers were cited as being critical to employee engagement' (MacLeod and Clarke, 2009a, 75). Using these four enablers as a lens to assess your activity, both as a manager and in the wider organisation, can help you understand what you need to do to authentically engage employees not just within formal training activities, but on a day-to-day basis. The enablers are not specific to the museum world; they are relevant to lots of different settings. However, I think they are particularly useful in the museum and heritage sector, where many people are attracted by value-based work.

In 2014, the authors of the original *Engage for Success* report published a new study looking at the links between performance, engagement and wellbeing. They proposed that the relationship between engagement and wellbeing form a 'virtuous circle': employees who enjoy high levels of wellbeing are highly engaged at work, and vice versa (MacLeod and Clarke, 2014, 15). In order to safeguard the wellbeing of employees, the report suggests including additional values in the enablers of engagement: 'support and good working relationships, plus well-designed jobs and working environments' (MacLeod and Clarke, 2014, 17).

In the modern museum, staff development isn't just about delivering a training course now and then. It's about a holistic culture of respect and integrity, and taking the wellbeing of your colleagues seriously.

Creating a training plan

When it comes to more formal engagement in the form of training and development, we need to look beyond the induction we discussed earlier. However, like the induction, a training plan for your Visitor Experience team should be well thought-out, align with organisational values and cater for a variety of needs and learning styles.

A good starting point for a training plan is to conduct a skills review. Involve your team in this. What necessary training do they feel they don't currently have? What would they like to know more about? What skills could they gain that would help them better engage with visitors?

This is also sometimes called a training needs analysis. There are lots of templates available online, but you can start by taking some time to think about the questions below:

1 What skills and competencies do your team need and what is their relative importance?
2 How do you measure levels of competence within your teams?
3 Where are your team currently in terms of the skills and competencies they need?
4 What training is available to help bridge any gaps?

For Visitor Experience teams, the logistics of training is always a tricky thing to solve. Time off the floor is always rare and precious for frontline teams; and in recent times of both recession and COVID-19, it is increasingly hard to safeguard. However, I would always advocate dedicated training time for Visitor Experience teams. When I was at the Natural History Museum (NHM), our rota meant that we were deliberately over-staffed on Tuesday, meaning staff could be freed up for training. I know most museums will not be able to manage something on this scale, but it's really important to try and set regular time aside, otherwise training will inevitably be short-term and unlinked to a bigger picture.

Remember that training and development doesn't always need to mean taking staff off the floor. Shorter briefing sessions can be used for quick, regular training interventions before the museum opens and buddying and shadowing schemes can be used for effective on-the-job training.

A strategic training plan should also speak to the vision of the organisation, prioritising the values and goals that the museum has identified as important. So, if your organisation has a value of being open and accessible to all, how is this exemplified in the training plan? Diversity training? Training to increase awareness of disabilities? Foreign language or sign language lessons? Another thing your training plan has to encompass is a variety of delivery methods in order to suit different learning styles. If all of your training is done in a lecture theatre, this is going to exclude some people who don't do well in that environment.

I think it's also important to give people choice in their own training and development. Although there are always going to be some topics that have to be covered, such as security or till training, there is no need to force people into learning about non-compulsory subjects they aren't interested in. Harnessing genuine enthusiasm for a topic is the best way to give a member of staff an enriching learning experience. They will also then be able to transmit that enthusiasm and knowledge to visitors, creating a better experience for all. This idea of harnessing authentic passion was what inspired me to create the training plan at the NHM, illustrated in Figure 14.1.

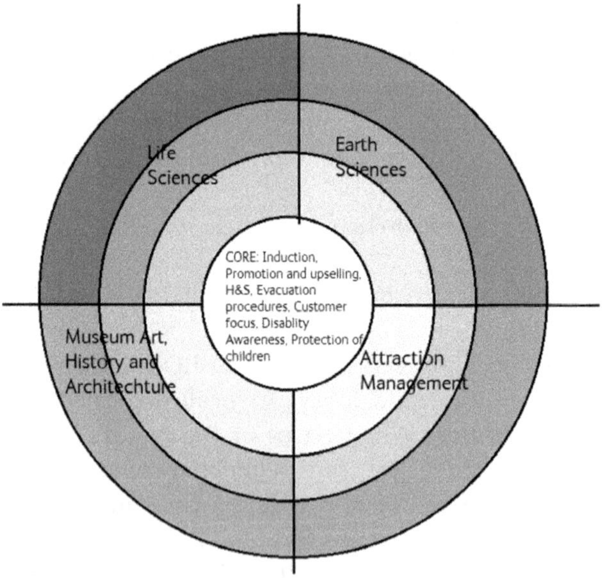

Figure 14.1 *NHM Training Wheel, 2014*

At its centre, our training wheel covered some core modules that every Visitor Assistant had to go through in order to be fully trained. This included induction, some compulsory organisation-wide courses and mandatory subjects such as diversity and data protection.

Once the team member had completed these core modules, they were able to choose one of four strands in which to continue their development. This enabled team members to navigate the huge number of disciplines covered at the NHM, and focus their efforts on an area that really interested them. The four strands included Earth Sciences (geology, palaeontology, mineralogy), Life Sciences (zoology, entomology, botany), the cultural history of the Museum (museology, social history) and finally Attractions Management (business, funding, management – this was designed for people who wanted to progress into non-collections museum management roles).

Allowing Visitor Assistants to self-select these strands meant that managers could assign courses to the relevant people, knowing that if we were running a behind-the-scenes tour in the Spirit Collection, for example, that the 'Life Sciences' group were prioritised for sign-up.

Then, as staff progressed through their time at the Museum, they would reach the outer rungs of the wheel, where we positioned more advanced self-led activities, such as preparing a training session themselves on a specialist subject or carrying out job shadowing with other departments.

This model accounted for the fact that not all Visitor Assistants planned to be with us long-term. We know that people join Visitor Experience teams for lots of different reasons. They might see it as a long-term career, they might want to progress elsewhere in the organisation, or they might simply be looking for a job that fits in with whatever else they are doing in their life. The training wheel allowed people to drive their own development; they got out what they put in. It also allowed people to develop their own interests and learn skills they needed to progress, whilst always bringing it back to the core purpose: engaging with our visitors.

Other museums have taken a similar approach in giving people choice about their training. At Cleveland Museum of Art in the USA, employees have to fulfil a certain amount of training hours. Although the number of hours is mandatory, employees have choice in how they are used. 'Employees can easily fulfil the requirement by choosing from a wide selection of workshops and lectures offered monthly – including such topics as diversity awareness, harassment in the workplace, conflict resolution, interviewing skills, training in CPR and how to use a fire extinguisher' (Lila Wallace – Reader's Digest Fund, 2000, 36).

Obviously, museums such as the NHM and the Cleveland Museum of Art have a significant budget and are lucky to have training sessions financed and safeguarded. But even in smaller museums, the training wheel concept can be applied. Self-led research and job-shadowing activities don't take much budget. They just take an open-minded approach from the rest of the museum staff and the willingness to support the development of our front-facing teams.

Visitor engagement training

Whatever shape your training plan takes, one thing it will certainly include is training staff in the all-important face-to-face engagement with visitors. Most organisations used to describe this as 'customer service', and I'm sure many still do. As discussed earlier in the book, I prefer the phrase 'visitor engagement', which I see as a much broader concept, encompassing the whole value of the interaction between staff and visitors.

In the introduction to this book, I described visitor engagement as being the 'soft' side of Visitor Experience. However, soft skills are not necessarily easy ones to hone, and visitor engagement really is a specialism. This isn't to say that it's unteachable. In the AIM *Success Guide to Visitor Experience*, Victoria Wallace, former CEO of Leeds Castle, says 'whilst it helps if your front of house team or volunteers are naturally sunny, happy people, do not forget that you can teach warmth' (Wallace, 2013). So, how do we teach our team to have excellent engagements with our visitors?

I think one of the key factors is not talking down to your team. Basic manners such as saying please and thank you are something that should be looked for at the recruitment stage, and if your team already have that, a training course will simply be teaching them something they already know. Remembering that visitor engagement really is a specialism; don't be afraid to go into depth. On my visitor engagement training courses, I talk about many of the things I have discussed in this book, from Falk's model of identity-related visitor motivation to audience segmentation and visitor mapping. I also talk about concepts in psychology, such as transactional analysis and conflict resolution. By engaging the team intellectually yet informally, I find that much more interesting discussions and debates arise, and we can get closer to the root of the dynamics of human interaction.

Doing a visitor mapping exercise with the team is my way of getting them to practise putting themselves in the visitors' shoes, which I think is a really important element of any visitor engagement training. Understanding and empathising with the visitor point of view will help the team anticipate and respond to visitor needs, and go above and beyond expectations. Other museums try different methods to achieve this. For example, the Museum of

London training plan (which is available online, Gillett, 2016) explains: 'The course starts by asking volunteers to think about their own experiences of receiving customer care in their everyday lives, and then moves on to help them consider how they can improve their own volunteer role in customer care in their museums' context.' You can find more ideas for getting staff to step into visitors' shoes in Chapter 11.

Another factor in successful visitor engagement training is a clear link to the aims of the organisation. This goes back to that first enabler of engagement described in *Engage for Success*: 'Strategic Narrative' (MacLeod and Clarke, 2009b). Not only should there be a clear organisational vision put forward by leadership, but all members of staff should know how they fit into that vision, and what part they can personally play in realising it. However, as we all know, organisational aims and values are generally couched in quite broad language. As Visitor Experience managers, it's our job to use visitor engagement training to clarify how those values can be translated into the day-to-day job of visitor-facing staff.

Table 14.2 is an example from the Customer Service Strategy I created for the NHM, explored more fully in Chapter 12. Although it's a few years old, I think it's a good example of translating the broad, 'management speak' of

Table 14.2 *NHM visitor-facing principles*

Museum value	Visitor-facing principles
Accessible	• We are friendly, approachable and proactive • We are clear and honest in our communication • We are inclusive and open to all, treating each visitor as an individual • We are flexible and adaptable
Expert	• We proactively share our knowledge about the Museum, engaging people with our purpose, collections, activities and services • We share knowledge across all teams, pooling our experience and delivering a consistent service • We take ownership for answering customers' questions • We are committed to continuously improving what we do • We design customer-centred processes, procedures and experiences designed to enable easy and seamless interactions with the Museum
Inspiring	• We take pride in representing the Museum and in our work • We confidently share our enthusiasm and passion for the Natural History Museum and the natural world • We encourage and enable people to engage with the Museum and all it has to offer • We work collaboratively with colleagues and other teams, enabling each other to deliver great customer service
Relevant	• We are proactive in adapting to situations • We actively listen to understand others' needs • We evolve our service and try new things to best meet our visitors' expectations • We seek to understand our visitors and personalise our interactions accordingly

organisational values into tangible actions and behaviours. I took the NHM values of the time, and translated them into a set of visitor-facing principles. This way, the Visitor Experience team could see that the actions they take on the floor every day contribute directly to how the Museum expresses itself.

The final point to mention when it comes to visitor engagement training is contracted staff. Many museums contract out part of their visitor operation and, accordingly, the staff who have a direct impact on the visitor experience. Looking at it from the visitor point of view, it seems completely weird that staff in the same museum would be trained differently: visitors can't see the organisational chart of the museum during their visit, and they wouldn't care if they could. That's why I rolled out the aforementioned Customer Service Strategy to all contract partners as well as directly employed NHM staff: it was worth the extra effort to ensure a seamless visitor experience.

This approach is also taken at the Cleveland Museum of Art in the USA. 'As part of its contract with the company that provides its restaurant services, the Cleveland Museum of Art requires the firm's employees who work at the museum to attend training. "To visitors, they're museum employees and how they interact with the public reflects on us," said Kate Sellers, the Museum's deputy director. In turn, Sellars said, the museum picks up half the wages of restaurant workers for the time spent in training sessions they are required to attend' (Lila Wallace – Reader's Digest Fund, 2000, 42).

When considering the roll-out of your visitor engagement training plan, therefore, remember to include everyone involved in the visitor experience, including those who don't directly work for you.

Continuing professional development (CPD)

In 2019 and 2020, a survey by grassroots Twitter group FOH Museums 'demonstrated consistently . . . that workers in Front of House roles are more likely to feel undervalued than their Back of House counterparts' (FOH Museums, 2020). FOH Museums put this feeling of being undervalued partially down to lack of access to training. Whilst job-related training is often available, such as the visitor engagement training discussed above, it's the opportunities for authentic continuing professional development (CPD) that are often lacking. FOH Museums say 'having the opportunity to gain deeper experiences within a museum specialism of interest, would be more beneficial to not only the individual but also the organisation as a whole.'

These CPD opportunities don't have to require a lot of budget. Job shadowing, talking to role models within the organisation (informational interviews), cross-organisational job swaps and self-led study are all cost-effective options. Although there are some logistical barriers to this, FOH

Museums has identified one glaring problem, in that 35% of front-of-house staff polled on Twitter said they didn't have access to one-to-one meetings with line managers regarding professional development. Again, this goes back to the *Engage for Success* enablers, and particularly the need for 'engaging managers' (MacLeod and Clarke, 2009b). As MacLeod and Clarke write, 'the relationship between a jobholder and their manager is key . . . it can make or break you' (MacLeod and Clarke, 2009b). Therefore take the time to meet individually with your team. Understand their long-term goals. Give honest feedback. Be realistic about how the museum can support their goals, and where possible, offer consistent support to help meet these goals. This doesn't mean spoon-feeding opportunities to everyone; it means coaching individuals to stretch themselves and keep themselves engaged.

CPD for visitor-facing teams doesn't need to cost the earth. The biggest resource required is your time, patience, support and passion for getting the best out of your team. The rewards are innumerable: staff retention, a happy and engaged team, talent development and colleagues who feel supported to progress within the organisation.

Case Study 14: Visitor engagement training at Tate

David Hingley, Head of Visitor Experience at Tate Britain and Tate Modern, has been working on a new engagement programme for visitor-facing staff that is designed to move the team's approach from 'service' to 'engagement'. As it is a programme that combines a contemporary approach to visitor engagement (any attempt to eradicate the word 'service' is fine by me), achievable professional development opportunities and a clear articulation of how organisational values are expressed in visitor engagement, it felt like the perfect case study for this chapter.

Showing how important it is to make training and development part of strategy, Hingley's engagement programme is built into the Visitor Experience future planning. For each quarter, Hingley has laid out not just the training objectives, but other developments that will support the team's evolution, such as building relationships with other departments and conducting mystery visits. The development of the team supports the broader agenda of the department and, likewise, cultural changes within the organisation will support the engagement of the team.

Hingley has defined visitor engagement for his team by redefining Tate's values in a way that describes how he wants staff to present to visitors, as Figure 14.2 on the next page shows.

At the heart of this practical application of this programme is a training package developed in conjunction with training consultancy The Whole Story.

The course, entitled 'Engage+', trains the visitor-facing team to ensure every conversation is better. Traditionally, visitor interactions have been seen as falling into one of four categories: revenue (e.g. selling someone a guidebook), security (e.g. asking someone not to touch something), help (e.g. giving directions) and engagement (e.g. talking to someone about a piece of art). Engage+ aims to add that extra engagement element into every conversation. For example:

TATE-WIDE VALUES	VISITOR CARE AND ENGAGEMENT BEHAVIOURS To help us create this experience, we need everyone who looks after our visitors to be:
KIND	**Welcoming** – we greet visitors as we encounter them within galleries, respond to their needs and act as brand ambassadors for Tate in everything we do. **Personal** – we are empathetic to the different types of visitors, their motivations and needs, and we adjust the way we interact with them accordingly. We bring our individual personalities to our interactions and we share our own perspectives on art. We add the personal element which a book or audio guide can't – and take that opportunity to enage our visitors.
OPEN	**Supportive** – we look after ourselves and our colleagues so we can best look after our visitors. We know who to call on for assistance. And we share and celebrate team success. **Conversational** – we proactively approach visitors and start an informal discussion with them about their general visit or art specifically.
BOLD	**Confident** – we are able to handle and resolve visitor-related issues and challenging situations by ourselves or, if required, by contacting managers for support.
RIGOROUS	**Enterprising** – we promote the whole Tate offer, and encourage visitors to join, buy or donate. We always consider 'how can I make this experience better?' and share ideas for improvement. We listen to visitors and pass on their comments. We take ownership of situations, and report presentation (or other) issues we cannot resolve ourselves. **Knowledgeable** – we continuously update our knowledge of Tate and the stories we tell, and of our processes and procedures. We are able to communicate everything we know appropriately to different visitors.

Figure 14.2 *Tate visitor care and engagement behaviours.* Source: David Hingley, 2022

Visitor asks:
'Where are the toilets?'
A HELP answer would be:
'They're just down here on your left'
An ENGAGE + answer would be:
'They're just down here on the left, and in this building you'll find them in the same place on every floor' or 'They're just down here on the left, you'll pass one of my favourite pieces on the way.'

Hingley says: 'I am really clear this isn't necessarily revolutionary, but providing a team with a common language to talk about interaction, means that we have a way of thinking about, and quantifying, whether the work we're doing is as good as we hope. I think this applies to all of us, at every level. I find myself leaving an interaction and asking myself "was that really engage plus, or was it only okay?" and I think that's how we ensure we constantly improve.'

On top of the Engage+ training course, Hingley's programme looks to introduce more professional development opportunities, such as cross-department working, cross-organisational learning and experience, the opportunity to support Tate research and apprenticeships. This, he hopes, will 'give people in front of house roles the opportunity that those in office-based jobs often take for granted. If your job is essentially to be accessible to visitors and operating in public for pretty much all your working hours – when do you really get time to think, network with sector colleagues, and see what's beyond what you do? We spend too long in the sector building our own versions of the same approach for front of house teams, when we could get a lot further, a lot faster by sharing opportunities across our teams and organisations.'

CHAPTER 15

Innovation and Visitor Experience Teams

> Innovation is not for geniuses working alone. It is a group activity.
>
> (Theodore Henderson, *Forbes*)

One of the most effective things that can be done to make sure your visitor experience is constantly evolving and improving is to foster a culture of innovation within your teams.

When we talk about innovation, the tech sector is probably the first thing that jumps to mind. Even when people talk about innovation in the museum sector, they often focus on technological advancement. For example, when describing the use of innovation by recipients of Art Fund money, an article in *The Guardian* in February 2022 talked about development of apps to make collections remotely accessible, interactive exhibits and the launch of virtual field trips (Bakare, 2022).

However, innovation doesn't necessarily have to mean high-tech and high-budget. Merriam-Webster simply defines innovation as 'introduction of something new', whether that be a device, method or idea (Merriam-Webster, 2022). So, you don't need to be Apple or Google to be an innovative organisation. You just need to be open to trialling new ideas.

The benefits of innovation

Innovation isn't something that should only happen in the board room. Great ideas can come from anywhere, and if you are looking to solve problems in your visitor operation, what better think tank than the people who work on the frontline of that operation every day? If you are open to innovation from all levels in your museum, you'll gain access to the wide range of knowledge and experience in all your employees.

Not only that, but fostering a culture of innovation has great benefits for employee engagement. By encouraging new ideas, you can demonstrate that you place value on the thoughts and suggestions of your team, and that you are willing to try things out to solve the problems that are important to them. People need to feel that they have agency in their work. For frontline teams, whose work is often restricted to specific locations and times, it's really important to find authentic opportunities to give them that. Being able to see an idea through from beginning to delivery is a great development opportunity for your employees, and we already know that if you can give your staff opportunities for genuine engagement, they are likely to stay engaged longer, and ultimately stay with you longer.

In my experience, because visitor-facing teams know the audience of a museum like nobody else, they will often come up with the most visitor-focused ideas. If something is impacting the visitor experience, it's impacting them, so it's worth their while to suggest and advocate a better way. Additionally, I have found that employees will be so much more engaged with an idea and invested in its success if it originated within their team. So, overall, you end up with a better visitor experience.

Finally, engendering a culture of innovation in your team can help you save money, because you are nurturing home-grown talent rather than paying for costly consultancy services. If you are transparent with your team about the challenges you are facing as an organisation, such as lack of budget, it gives people clear boundaries and an idea of what problems need solving. They will often come up with cost-effective suggestions as a result. You'll read about a clear example of this in the case study.

Fostering a culture of innovation

In the previous chapter, we looked at the four pillars of employee engagement from *Engage for Success* (MacLeod and Clarke, 2009b):

- strategic narrative
- engaging managers
- employee voice
- organisational integrity.

These pillars are also crucial in fostering a culture of innovation. Museums must have a strategic narrative that employees can buy into. Staff members at all levels should feel invited to take part in furthering the goals of the organisation. They need to have engaging managers who care about their ideas and support their input. They need to have agency in solving problems they come across; to have their voice not only heard but listened to. Finally, museums should have organisational integrity in being serious about supporting employee innovation. When they ask for ideas and input, they should mean it.

How can we put all of that into action in our museums?

1. Be open about the challenges faced

When encouraging innovation in Visitor Experience teams it's important to be transparent. You can't expect team members to be passionate about solving problems they don't know exist. Whether your problem is a dwindling audience, lack of diversity, falling income or tricky logistics, involve your team. Managers are not expected to automatically have the answer to every problem.

It's also important to be realistic about what can be done, and what is out of your control. So, if there is no budget to carry out new ideas, be honest about that. Ensure your team know the parameters in which they can operate. Can they make decisions that impact conservation? Can they have time off the floor to work up a trial? Do they have a good understanding of security? At Historic Royal Palaces, we encourage staff to feel empowered to make decisions on the floor – as long as they consider the three S's: safety, security and spend.

2. Understand that ideas can come from anywhere

Although some museums might have specific people whose job it is to come up with great museums, most will not. Because we rarely have the luxury of a paid 'innovator', it's important to realise that innovation can come from anywhere. Visitor Experience team members make great innovators, for all the reasons I've described above. So it's important, for museum managers to be open and receptive to new ideas, whatever department or level they come from.

Innovation is also not a solo activity. According to Theodore Henderson, writing for *Forbes* magazine: 'Innovation is not for geniuses working alone. It is a group activity and definitely a teachable skill' (Henderson, 2017). I really love that sentiment because I do feel that innovation is best accomplished with others. Whenever I have a tricky problem that needs solving, I don't try and tackle it alone. Instead, I'll park it in my brain till I can sit and chat it through with colleagues, knowing that the conversation will spark new ideas and that together we'll crack it.

Finally, a diverse workforce is crucial in driving innovation. A *Forbes* survey showed that 85% of respondents believed 'a diverse and inclusive workforce is crucial to encouraging different perspectives and ideas that drive innovation' (Egan, 2015). Only by welcoming all backgrounds, experience and ideas will you be able to bring together the tools you need to innovate for new challenges.

3. Create resource to encourage innovation

In Visitor Experience, we can sometimes slip into reactive mode; constantly firefighting and coping with the competing demands of visitors and other departments, so that there is no time to pause, reflect or plan. This sort of operation creates a really hostile environment for innovation. Although necessity can sometimes be the mother of invention (we saw this particularly in the COVID-19 pandemic) this sort of innovation is usually short-term, based on adapting to new circumstances and ultimately aiming to revert to the status quo rather than trying to create the circumstances of the future.

If you want to foster innovation, you have to give your employees the time and space to think about the bigger picture. Companies such as Google have formalised this by adopting a '20% rule', encouraging staff to spend 20% of their working time on innovation (Livescault, 2022). This approach is rarely adopted outside the tech industry, and is hardly realistic for frontline museum staff, but it shows how important time and space is. Building in some time to think, whether it's a reflective briefing at the end of the day, a regular training and development day or even an annual away day, will help your staff detach from the busy operation and day-to-day tasks and focus on innovation.

As well as time and space, innovation can also require budget. This doesn't mean spending thousands of pounds on product development, but even taking staff off the floor to develop a new idea does equate to spending. For museums on a shoestring, this can be difficult to budget for. However, I have come across a couple of examples that build innovation into the annual budget, making planning and forecasting easier.

One was a customer service training scheme across several weeks for Visitor Assistants. At the end of their course, which was already budgeted as essential training, participants were asked to come up with a new idea for the visitor offer. The best one was chosen and trialled, with the understanding that staffing resource would be allowed to complete this. Another idea was a presentation format, where staff were encouraged to submit new income generation ideas to a panel of management. Budget was set aside to trial successful ideas, ideally (but not always) offset by the new income generated.

Although innovation doesn't always require budget, it's a good way of showing staff you are serious about incentivising creative thinking: you're putting your money where your mouth is.

4. Trial and experiment

In 2001, a new style of project management known as the 'Agile' methodology was developed by software manufacturers (Dingsøyr et al., 2012, 1). The Agile process eschews the documentation-heavy approach of other methodologies to create a lean, flexible and adaptive approach to designing and launching new products. Although it was created for the field of software development, many of the principles can be applied to any audience-focused product, including the museum visitor experience.

One of the core ideas of Agile is that change can happen at any time (Dingsøyr et al., 2012, 2). An idea is developed and launched not once but many times, and teams learn and adapt their practice based on customer feedback. This is highly relevant to the visitor experience. Like a piece of software, the visitor operation is a highly complex model, and it can often be hard to predict what impact a small change will have. A trial-and-error approach helps us learn and ultimately come up with the best outcome.

Visitor feedback is also central to Agile. In museums, although we can plan new visitor offers and operations in the boardroom for months, it often isn't until we take an idea live, with actual visitors, that we can understand its success or failure. This is why so many Visitor Experience Managers advocate the use of 'soft launches' or trials of new experiences with friendly test groups. For example, I invited sector colleagues to be the test group when we opened the Great Pagoda at Kew, and a new exhibition at Kew Palace. This helped us sense-check things like capacities, visitor flow and dwell time.

5. Accept and destigmatise failure

An inevitable outcome of experimentation is failure. If your organisation encourages innovation, it must be open to and accepting of the idea that sometimes it won't work out. Yet fear of failure remains a huge barrier to risk-taking, not just in the museum world but in many sectors. In an environment where we laud every achievement on LinkedIn, it can be hard to admit when things haven't worked out so well. However, failure is rarely the end of the world, and is always an opportunity to learn.

When I was working at the Natural History Museum (NHM), I came up with a great idea to join forces with the other museums in South Kensington to put an information station in the tunnel from South Kensington tube station. This could help visitors plan their visits and make informed decisions as they head towards the 'museumopolis' that is the V&A, NHM and the Science Museum. We could let visitors know the queue times at the various sites and advise them what not to miss. Brilliant idea, right? I gathered some colleagues from the Science Museum and the V&A and we went to check out possible locations in the tunnel. However, it quickly became obvious that the idea didn't have legs. Visitors rushed past us, unwilling to stop and chat, oblivious to everything apart from the signs to the museums. I had to turn, shamefaced, to my colleagues and admit that the idea had been something of a damp squib.

A failure, then. But what had really been lost? Half an hour of our time, maybe, but even that was better than committing more resource to a more developed version of the idea; something that we might have done if we hadn't carried out our mini-trial first. Plus, I gained something. First, the idea made me initiate contact with my colleagues at the other museums: something we weren't good enough at doing in those days. Secondly, I gained a deeper understanding about visitors; that when they are dead set on reaching their destination, the best thing we can do to help is really clear, directional signage. More detailed visit planning has to come later. So although failure can often seem like a waste of time at best, and a professional embarrassment at worst, there is always something to be gained.

6. Recognise and reward innovation

When innovation does happen, it's really important to both recognise this and reward it. Even if ideas don't go all the way to fruition, it's crucial to acknowledge that a staff member has contributed the idea in the first place, and reward the culture that allows innovation to happen.

In 2022, a Visitor Host came to me at Kew Palace with an idea. Why not put a glass case with historic clothes in the old wardrobe we have on the second floor? Unfortunately, I had to explain that the idea wasn't going to work: for one thing, the environmental conditions on the second floor are not stable enough to house historic collections. But I took on board her suggestion that we should do more to interpret that wardrobe, and congratulated her on the idea. Taking the time to have that conversation in full meant that the member of staff understood more about the conservation parameters we have to work within; so her next idea will probably be even better. She also heard that her idea was encouraged and knows that her future thoughts and suggestions will be listened to.

Where ideas do get trialled and are a success, there's nothing more important than publicly celebrating it. Not only does this reward those who had the ideas and delivered them; it encourages others and shows that your organisation welcomes innovative thinking.

Case Study 15: The Eurovision Song Contest Exhibition and Innri Hringur

I'm using another case study from my own experience here because I think it's a great example of an idea being generated collaboratively with frontline teams, and going on to have a big impact on the visitor experience.

In my spare time, I do some work for a tiny museum in Iceland that's very close to my heart: the Eurovision Song Contest Exhibition in Húsavík. This new museum sprang up as a response to the huge cult following gained by the 2020 Netflix movie, *Eurovision Song Contest: the story of Fire Saga*, which was set and filmed in Húsavík.

The museum tells the story of the *Fire Saga* movie, as well as the Contest itself and specifically, Iceland's extremely enthusiastic but so far (at the time of writing) unsuccessful participation in Eurovision. Like many of Iceland's museums, it's small, quirky and thoroughly charming. After months of working with the Húsavík team remotely, in August 2020 I finally got the opportunity to go out to Iceland and work on the museum. I went there intending to offer my services and expertise; but actually, I came away full of inspiration and a hundred ideas to implement at the site I was looking after at the time, Kew Palace.

More than anything, it was the philosophy of the place that inspired me. The team at Húsavík couldn't have been more open and welcoming; not just to me but to the tourists who flocked to the adjoining hotel and bar wanting a sneak peek at the unfinished exhibition. *Fire Saga* has unleashed a whole new legion of Eurovision fans into the world; and many of them had braved COVID-19 restrictions and testing regimes to make their way to Húsavík, the home of the movie. When they saw that an exhibition about their new favourite subject was under way, they were desperate to see behind the scenes, and the exhibition team were only too happy to let them, building site or not!

This philosophy, which I eventually came to term *innri hringur* (Icelandic for 'inner circle') was expressed in other ways. The team talked openly to visitors about the development of the project, listened to ideas and suggestions, and even acted on many of them. Visitors didn't feel that they were being 'allowed in', in the way that we sometimes talk about 'allowing access' to museums and historic sites. Instead, they were being invited in as equals. Eurovision passion demolished any hierarchy between staff and visitors; everyone was entirely on the same page. I loved it. We so often talk about removing barriers for visitors, but here it was in action: a total democratisation of the visitor experience.

I returned to London fully in love, not only with Húsavík, but with the philosophy of *innri hringur*. I wanted to try it out at Kew Palace, but how? Royal Palaces are built on the very principle of 'us' and 'them'. Hierarchy is at the core of their existence. Plus, most of the objects we display come from the Royal Collection; literally the Royal Family's own stuff. How could we invite visitors to get as up close and personal as we had in Húsavík?

I presented my Húsavík experience to my Host team and asked them to think about how we could implement *innri hringur* here at Kew. They came back with a brilliant idea: Hidden Spaces tours. These would be an informal alternative to our more formal evening tours. At the end of the day, we would invite small groups of visitors into the parts of the Palace that are normally out of bounds: our Tudor undercroft and our attics. The tours would be conversational and intimate in tone, and best of all, they would cost the Palace nothing. The Hosts had realised that in the last half hour of the day, we always had one extra Host on duty because the breaks have finished.

Although the idea didn't necessarily come fully formed, within a few minutes of conversation we had fleshed it out into a workable idea; great evidence that innovation really is a group activity. I knew it was important to trial this quickly and build on the momentum the team had built up. I quickly wrote a risk assessment, figured out the ticketing, organised some training and we trialled it that same week.

I loved this idea so much, not just because it was a great visitor offer, but because the team had really embraced the idea of *innri hringur*. They had taken my presentation and used it as a springboard for innovation. They had also used their knowledge of our then precarious financial situation: the tours would generate income, without costing us a penny. Being so transparent with the team about our budgets had really paid off.

The tours were an instant success, and even went on to win an award for creative commerce at the Cultural Enterprises awards. It was fantastic to have the achievement and innovation of the team realised in that way; it really had been driven by them. For me, this is a great example of a team working within the parameters they have been set to innovate, and delivering an outcome that demonstrably improved the visitor experience at Kew Palace.

CHAPTER 16

Change Management

> Being armed with an understanding of the context means that you're much more likely to develop a plan of action that will land successfully.
>
> (Claire Lane, The Ashmolean Museum)

In Part 3 of this book, we've talked a lot about developing the visitor experience. An unavoidable part of this development is organisational change, and taking your visitor offer or your visitor-facing teams from where they are now to where you want them to be. Change management is a huge topic, and one that many books have focused on in detail. But as change is such a crucial part of making visitor experiences better, I think it's important to talk about it here. In this chapter, you won't find an in-depth discussion of change management or an exhaustive list of change models. You will find, however, an overview of what change management is, and an exploration of how some of the most popular models and techniques can be utilised when managing change around the visitor experience.

What is change management?

'Change' in the Visitor Experience setting can mean many things, including:

- opening a new exhibition or experience
- closing a space temporarily or permanently
- internal team restructures
- changes in working conditions, such as hours, uniform or benefits
- stopping a programme, such as tours, or starting a new one.

However, it can also include any type of change; big or small. The Association for Project Management (APM) defines change management as 'a structured approach to moving an organisation from the current state to the desired future state' (APM, 2017, 5). The reason the APM advocates a 'structured approach' to the bit in between the current state and the desired future state is that it's by far the most complex part. If you lead a Visitor Experience team, you might think that you should be able to drive change just by articulating it. Unfortunately, most of us know that is almost never the case. Or, you might think that your background of operating in the ever-changing, unpredictable world of Visitor Experience gives you all the skills you need to manage change without the help of a formal model. After all, the APM itself states in its *Introduction to Change Management*: 'Good [change] project managers are men and women who have the judgement and experience to manage conflicting stakeholders' aims and objectives and act effectively in the face of a constant stream of unpredictable problems' (APM, 2017, vi). Sounds a lot like Visitor Experience, doesn't it?

However, research shows that most change management efforts, including those in Visitor Experience organisations, do not fully succeed (APM, 2017, 2). Part of the reason for this is often that managers have not taken the time to appreciate the complex context and intricate stakeholder relationships surrounding the change they wish to create. Change models can help us avoid this pitfall by giving us a map that ensures we make all the stops we need to on the way to our destination.

This is not to say that a good model can solve everything. Soft skills are so important in change management, and there is no model that can help you through the change process if you're just not a people person at heart. As the APM says, 'Good project managers know that formal project management tools on their own are not sufficient to ensure a successful outcome' (APM, 2017, v). Luckily, if you already work in Visitor Experience, chances are you already have those soft skills. Taking some hints and tips from the popular change models out there can only increase your chances of embedding change and succeeding in your developments. So, with that in mind, let's explore some change models.

Models for change

There are many varieties of change models out there, and you may want to use a different one for different projects depending on your needs. However, if we look at a few of the most popular models, we can soon see that there are certain commonalities, and this may give an indication of what elements of the change management process are universally considered to be the most important.

The first model we'll look at is John Kotter's eight-stage process for successful organisational transformation. Kotter's stages run as follows:

1 Create urgency
2 Form a powerful coalition
3 Create a vision for change
4 Communicate the vision
5 Empower action
6 Create quick wins
7 Build on the change
8 Make it stick. (Kotter, 1996)

In this process, you can see that no active change occurs anywhere in the first four stages. Half of the model is focused on preparation for change, underlining Kotter's belief that a lot of groundwork has to be undertaken before change can occur. We also see an emphasis on embedding change. Kotter encourages us to 'build' on change in order to 'make it stick'. The APM agrees, saying 'until new behaviours are rooted in social norms and shared, values, they are subject to degradation as soon as the pressure for change is removed' (APM, 2017, 7). Complex change management is always a long-term project.

Another model that places emphasis on the before and after stages of change management is Kurt Lewin's 'Unfreeze, Change, Refreeze' model, first posited back in 1947 (Lewin, 1947). Here, equal emphasis is put on all three stages, showing that as much work has to be done in preparing and embedding change as in delivering the change itself. In fact, according to the APM:

> . . . the Unfreezing stage is probably one of the more important stages to understand in the world of change we live in today. This stage is about getting ready to change. It involves getting to a point of understanding that change is necessary and getting ready to move away from our current comfort zone. The first stage is about preparing ourselves, or others, before the change.
>
> (APM, 2017, 8)

Lewin's model is obviously some decades old, and some ideas around change have evolved (APM, 2017, 8). One of the key areas of Lewin's model that might be understood differently today is the idea of 'Refreezing'. Whilst Lewin sees change as a process of leaving one status quo and returning to a new, but static, status quo, we now understand change as more of a constant evolution. In a world that seems to be transforming at an increasingly high speed, change really is the only constant.

In 1990 Michael Beer, along with colleagues Eisenstart and Spector, developed a six-step change management model. The steps focus on assessing the change needs, or creating an 'accurate diagnosis' (Stouten, Rousseau and

De Cremer, 2018, 755), articulating a clear vision, building a consensus, implementing change through collaboration, cementing change, and finally reviewing the change and making adjustments where necessary.

Another process model is Kanter, Stein and and Jick's 'Ten Commandments', which articulate the following steps:

1. 'Analysis of the organisation and the need for change
2. The creation of a shared vision
3. Separation of the past
4. Creating a sense . . . that important change is needed
5. Strong leader role
6. Political sponsorship is sought
7. Development of an implementation plan
8. Enabling structures... put into place
9. Change communication should be open and honest
10. Change needs to be reinforced and institutionalised' (Stouten, Rousseau and De Cremer, 2018, 755)

Like Kotter and Lewin, both the Beer and Kanter models emphasise the preparation stage of change management. They also both advocate a shared clarity of vision. Creating a clear vision for change, as well as ensuring everyone buys into that vision, is a really important part of change management. When I've pushed for change in my teams, especially when I'm asking staff to behave in a different way, such as being more commercially minded and developing their skills around promoting events or selling guidebooks, I've found it really helps people to understand why you are asking them to change. This should be really transparent and really clear. I don't see any downside in sharing financial details with the staff you want to action change. Sharing our site P&L (Profit and Loss) with my Host team at Kew Palace helped them understand the precarious financial position the organisation was in after the COVID-19 pandemic, and highlighted how the actions they took every day could really make an impact.

'People are more likely to accept change if they understand why it is happening, what it will entail and how it will affect them' says the APM. 'Individual change projects and programmes must be aligned with the overall strategy of the business and co-ordinated to create a manageable "picture" of change' (APM, 2017, 27). This goes back to the four pillars of employee engagement discussed in previous chapters: ensuring that staff can see there is no gap between what the organisation says and what it does. If that's the case, trust is built, which provides a strong and stable foundation for change to happen.

The final model I wanted to share was recommended to me by Claire Lane, Commercial Director at the Ashmolean Museum, whom you will meet in the case study at the end of this chapter. I find this model (Figure 16.1) really useful for carrying out that preparation phase, and making sure you have thought about every angle before you get stuck in to delivering the change. I also like that it's presented as a wheel, or map, rather than a process, affording you the flexibility to consider the issues in the way that works best for your organisation or project.

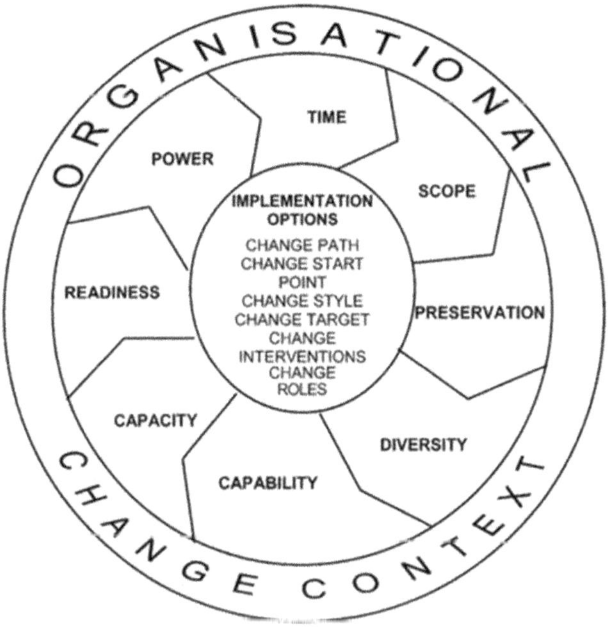

Figure 16.1 *Balogun and Hope-Hailey's Change Kaleidoscope.* Source: Hope-Hailey and Balogun, 2002

As Lane explains:

> . . . the idea here is that before you've started any of the change, you think about the context you're currently in. The outer ring features the elements you should give some pre-thought to, such as power, time and capacity. Are these elements enablers of the change (i.e. are they supportive) or are they going to be a constraint? Are there things you need to address before implementing? . . . The idea is that having understood your change context sufficiently, you can then determine the most appropriate way to navigate the points in the centre.
>
> (Lane, 2022)

Practically speaking, I find this model especially useful for planning the timeline of change. Often, we'll be working to a timescale for change to be delivered and we need to make sure that it's reasonable to fit the work required into that time. I'll use the template shown in Figure 16.1 to sketch out all of the considerations, such as research needed, departments that need to deliver dependencies or people who need to be consulted, and then use that information to plan in a timeline and make sure everything hangs together. By doing this, you can make sure everything happens at the right time, and you don't end up consulting key stakeholders too late into the change project.

Through synthesis of all of these change models, we can see that many of the points broadly fall into the following categories outlined by the APM (2017, 6): 'Assess – Prepare – Plan – Implement – Sustain'. So, even if you're not sure which model to go for, making sure you carry out activity in each of these five areas should help you plan for long-lasting change.

Whichever model you choose, driving change in Visitor Experience teams will always involve some element of managing people. So next, let's explore some ways of supporting staff through change.

Managing staff through change

Everyone reacts to change differently. Some people in your team will be ready to passionately embrace the change you want to create; others will resist. Some may be fearful or distrustful of the unknown; some may be worried about their skills and experience matching up to the changes.

As part of understanding the context around change, and preparing the ground, it's really important to get a thorough appreciation of different viewpoints. The APM advises change makers to 'spend time to really understand stakeholders – their perspectives and motivations. Ensure two-way communication, talk the stakeholders' language, seek feedback, listen, build relationships and trust. Communication alone does not guarantee engagement' (APM, 2017, 30). This can be harder in Visitor Experience teams, where logistics mean it's often difficult to get people off the floor for one-to-one conversations. But if this means the change plan takes a bit longer to deliver, it's absolutely worth it. If you don't do this groundwork at the start, you'll regret it later.

Taking on feedback from others doesn't mean agreeing with every viewpoint and twisting your plans to make everyone happy: you'll never establish long-term, positive change that way. Instead, it's important to know what you are dealing with; to identify people who might be able to champion change, who might need a bit more convincing and who are likely to act as barriers. This can help you tailor your plans and communications accordingly.

For example, if staff are worried that their skills sets won't meet the requirements of the change, you can ensure plenty of training is built into the delivery plan. If people are losing something they value, such as a space or activity they really love, just making sure you are creating space for people to articulate the emotional impact of the change, and acknowledging their loss, can go a long way.

One way to shepherd positive change with a team is to be very clear about what benefits the change will bring to them. Whether it's professional or personal development, a smoother visitor journey or increasing financial stability, make sure people have something tangible they can aim for. They have to know why the change is good.

Sometimes, however, change isn't good. It's hard to focus on the individual benefits of negative change programmes such as restructures or redundancies. Yes, it may mean a more stable or more efficient future for the organisation as a whole, but it's hard to spin that as a positive for the individual who is losing their job. In scenarios like this, I've found that whilst there isn't much you can say to make the situation better, there is a whole lot that can make things worse, such as poor communication, lack of consultation, lack of empathy, lack of support and training as staff prepare to leave the organisation and a lack of planning. These can be some of the most difficult transitions to manage (especially if you're delivering change that has been imposed upon you), and as a manager you can never make it truly better. The best you can do is make it fair, open and empathetic. Again, as a Visitor Experience manager, your soft skills are crucial here.

A really important thing to consider when managing negative change (or even just change that people are experiencing as negative) is where people might be on the change curve. The change curve was developed in the 1960s by Elisabeth Kübler-Ross, and I've found it really useful when managing the most serious change. The names of the stages can vary depending on what version you look at, but broadly speaking they fall into these categories:

1 shock and denial
2 anger
3 bargaining
4 depression
5 acceptance (Kübler-Ross Foundation, 2023).

People can move through this process (usually represented as a curve) at different paces, and they can also move back a stage, so it's important to realise that not everyone will be in the same place at the same time.

I remember having to give a Visitor Experience team news of redundancy, and then being surprised at how well they took it. Of course, I quickly realised that this wasn't their final reaction, and that this strange sense of euphoria they were exhibiting on being told the news was simply part of that first shock/denial reaction. By realising that, I was able to prepare myself for what was to come, which included a lot of anger. So, through utilising the change curve, we can start to understand where people are, meet them there, and try to support them successfully through the process towards acceptance.

Measuring change

Even if it is blatantly obvious to you that a change programme has been a success (and it may not be), it's really important to measure the change. Key to this is that planning stage, where you should set clear goals and objectives. As a reminder, SMART objectives are:

- Specific
- Measurable
- Achievable
- Relevant
- Timely.

In the initial stages of the process, measuring success allows you to make quick changes based on trials or feedback. It also allows you to demonstrate, not just to yourself and your team, but to other stakeholders, whether the objectives have been achieved. Because of this, the process carries risk. If you haven't achieved what you were aiming for, this failure may be exposed (APM, 2017, 33). However, the rewards can be huge. Delivering improvements in Visitor Experience is not only great for staff and visitors in the short run; success in this area can give you and your department credibility and leverage, providing evidence that when you are given the power to improve the Visitor Experience, you make it happen!

The thinking around measuring success should be happening in the planning stages of your change; it shouldn't be an afterthought. You have to consider many factors, such as the context of change and stakeholder perspective (APM, 2017, 36); in fact, many of the same areas discussed in the Balogun and Hope-Hailey's Change Kaleidoscope. Have a think about those areas and how you will define success in each one. Then, think about the best way to measure that. Will you conduct staff surveys? Look at retail figures? Try and use a mixture of qualitative and quantitative methods to gain a clear, overall picture, and if you need some tips about measuring change from the visitor point of view, why not go back to Chapter 12 of this book?

Finally, be aware that not all change is immediate. The APM advise change managers to 'be clear on how long key performance indicators will be measured for – not all outcomes will be achieved straight away and most benefits are realised months or even years after implementation' (APM, 2017, 39).

Case Study 16: National Trust pre-booking

A great example of a change manager who has utilised many of the above models in her work is Claire Lane, currently Commercial Director at the Ashmolean Museum in Oxford. In her current role, as well as previous roles at the National Trust and John Lewis, she has extensive experience of using change management to drive commercial improvements and innovation.

As this chapter has shown, there are many different options for those looking for an effective change management model, but for Lane, assessing and appreciating the wider context is key. 'Understanding the situation, the organisation's change context and the constraints and enablers is key to understanding the type of change an organisation is *able* to undertake alongside an understanding of the type of change it *wants* to undertake,' she explains. 'Applying Balogun and Hope-Hailey's Change Kaleidoscope will enable you to identify any constraints you may have to consider or address. It will also enable you to understand both the type of change you're seeking and the nature of change that's most appropriate. Armed with this understanding, you can work through your implementation options: the path you want to navigate, the change style that's most appropriate, what change interventions you're going to put into place and the roles you're going to need to implement it. And here, some of the more traditional process of change models can then really help. Being armed with an understanding of the context means that you're much more likely to develop a plan of action that will land successfully.'

Lane used this approach when, in 2020, she was working for the National Trust at the height of the pandemic. One of the teams Lane managed looked after events bookings; an area that was to scale up significantly as lockdown restrictions lessened and reopening was being considered. In order to maintain social distancing when the sites reopened, advance booking was to be introduced at over 200 properties. When planning for this huge change of activity, Lane was careful to take a wide view, using the Change Kaleidoscope to understand all the factors at play. Table 16.1 on the next page shows how Lane considered the various Change Kaleidoscope elements and applied them to the National Trust project:

As Lane explains 'the change context consisted mainly of enablers. There weren't many constraints, so we then utilised a more traditional process of change model to think about our implementation.'

'We formed a powerful guiding coalition – with a strong project team and steering group.

- We had a clear vision and scope.
- The project team were empowered to act on that vision and devise the implementation plan.

Table 16.1 *Change Kaleidoscope exercise (National Trust).* Source: Lane, 2022

Change Kaleidoscope element	National Trust application
Time	'There was very little time, which was both an enabler and a constraint. An enabler in that there was a sense of urgency. A constraint in that we didn't have the luxury of time to plan the perfect systems/processes/change path. We had three weeks to get all properties reopened on a bookable basis. There wasn't time to create perfection: we had to create something that worked as a minimum-viable product that we could then build on and improve over time in an agile way.'
Scope	'We were very clear on our scope: we had to introduce bookings for all properties to reopen as quickly as possible. This clarity was an enabler of the change.'
Preservation	'Other operating principles needed to be preserved i.e., our till operating and payment procedures/membership scanning functionality, etc. This wasn't an enabler or a constraint but we did need to think about how these systems would impact the visitor experience on the day.'
Diversity & Capability	'We brought together a diverse, cross-team working group to solve the challenge. We needed skill sets for every stage in the process: experts from our property teams, experts on the system we utilised to extract data from property teams, experts on the booking system, experts on our website to make sure the website featured the very latest information for supporters, IT infrastructure experts who could monitor website performance to make sure it could take the high volumes of supporters now visiting the website on a weekly basis to book, analytics experts to ensure we had the data we needed. We had a diverse and capable team; these were major enablers.'
Capacity	'We ensured that those working on the project were able to focus on it, given its criticality; this was an enabler.'
Readiness	'Preparation for change, stakeholder management, strong sponsorship and emphasising why there's a need for change are all absolutely critical for ensuring that an organisation is ready for change. We spent time on this and continued to do so as the project progressed; this was an enabler.'

- We communicated the vision, scope and implementation plan with all stakeholders with two-way conversations, listening closely to address any concerns, amending and improving our plans as well as securing engagement and support.
- We had some short-term wins and check points, adding additional properties in a staggered manner and monitoring progress closely with customer feedback loops. Some lovely feedback on social media about the great days out people were having really helped the team to keep pushing on, adding more properties, timeslots and capacity.

- We identified where improvements were necessary and implemented those improvements on an ongoing basis.
- We communicated, involved people and were honest with teams and stakeholders throughout.'

As identified in the Kaleidoscope exercise, the significant time constraints meant that the team were not aiming for a flawless completion of the project first time out. However, this isn't necessary a negative, as it allows for evolution and flexibility further down the line. Indeed, this is exactly why the review and amend stages of change management processes are so important: feedback is critical. As Lane explains:

'The booking system we had on launch wasn't perfect, but it worked in that we had it up and running in less than three weeks with more than 200 properties operating on a bookable basis and therefore able to reopen. With the luxury of more time, we then worked to secure a system that was more appropriate for operating bookings on an ongoing basis. As we've moved out of COVID-19, it became apparent that the booking system had significantly benefited some of the smaller properties and supporter feedback on the visitor experience at those properties suggested to us that it would be beneficial to keep some of the smaller properties on a booking system year-round. So, a year later we removed the majority of properties from the booking system to bring back the spontaneity some of our supporters were looking for – but kept a number of our smaller properties on the booking system to optimise the visitor experience at those properties.'

Through this case study, we can see that change isn't about following a process letter-by-letter, it's about using the tools these models suggest to help us better understand and utilise our own environments. As Lane says, 'it's about examining different change situations and contexts to consider the most appropriate interventions and how they are synchronised and phased through time. Applying the Change Kaleidoscope to whatever change scenario you're facing into will help you to understand the organisational change context – and then you can think about the most appropriate implementation options open to you: the path, the change style, the interventions and the roles.'

So, by fully appreciating the context of change, you are more likely to be successful in supporting your teams, and ultimately, developing your visitor experience.

Conclusion

In 2010, I attended my first Museums Association conference in Brighton. I was a new Visitor Experience Manager, keen to learn more, and I vividly remember my disappointment when I realised there was nothing on the conference agenda that spoke to my area of interest. Nothing about front-of-house staff, nothing about experience creation, nothing about the nuts and bolts of the visitor operation. Visitor Experience was seen as the way into a museum career, rather than a specialism in itself.

More than a decade later, I'm delighted that this viewpoint has changed. Today, the Museum Association has been part of creating a front-of-house charter of best practice, and Visitor Experience topics make regular appearances on conference agendas and in museum journals. For me, this is thrilling progress; an acknowledgement of how important the Visitor Experience is in ensuring museums really are for everyone. If any doubts do still exist about the value of this discipline, I see it as my job, and the job of my fellow specialists, to shine a light on what we do and keep it high on the agenda.

I wrote this book with the intention of sharing best practice and guidance in delivering fantastic visitor experiences. I was driven by the knowledge that Visitor Experience really is a specialism; it takes skill, knowledge and talent to pull it off.

So, to all my fellow Visitor Experience specialists: I hope you've been inspired by the case studies shared in this book to continue developing your own practice. I can't wait to see what you all do.

Now, have you thought about the toilets?

References and Further Reading

AC – NMW (Amgueddfa Cymru – National Museum Wales) (2018) *Visitor Experience Strategy 2018–2021*, https://museum.wales/media/48964/Visitor-Experience-Strategy.pdf. Accessed 29 April 2022.

ACE (Arts Council England) (2017) *Making a Shift Report: Disabled People and the Arts and Cultural Sector Workforce in England*, www.artscouncil.org.uk/sites/default/files/download-file/ACE206%20MAKING%20A%20SHIFT%20Report%20FINAL.pdf. Accessed 20 February 2022.

ACE (Arts Council England) (2019) *Equality, Diversity and the Creative Case*, www.artscouncil.org.uk/sites/default/files/download-file/Diversity_report_1718.pdf. Accessed 20 February 2022.

Aiken, J. (2007) Preparing for a National Emergency: The Committee on Conservation of Cultural Resources 1939–1944, *The Library Quarterly: Information, Community, Policy*, **77**, 275.

AIM (Association of Independent Museums) (2021) How to Make the Most of the Gift of Volunteering, https://aim-museums.co.uk/volunteering. Accessed 3 December 2021.

APM (Association for Project Management) (2017) *Introduction to Managing Change*, Princes Risborough.

Atkinson, C., Yates, D. and Brooke, N. (2020) Now That You Mention It, Museums Probably are a Target, *Museum Management and Curatorship*, **35**, 109–24.

Audience Agency (2021a) Audience Spectrum, https://theaudienceagency.org/audience-spectrum. Accessed 6 November 2021.

Audience Agency (2021b) Visitor Journey Mapping, https://theaudienceagency.org/services/visitor-journey-mapping. Accessed 20 February 2021.

Bakare, L. (2022) UK Museums Turn to Innovation to Keep Doors Open in Times of Covid, *The Guardian*, www.theguardian.com/culture/2020/aug/15/uk-museums-turn-to-innovation-to-keep-doors-open-in-times-of-covid. Accessed 25 February 2022.

Baldwin, J. (2022) Interview conducted by author, 17 March 2022.

Banecker, G. (2020) Capacity Managing your Entire Attraction is the New Normal after COVID-19, *Blooloop*, https://blooloop.com/museum/opinion/capacity-management-attractions-post-covid-19. Accessed 3 May 2021.

Beard, M. (2020) Front of House in the British Museum, *The TLS*, www.the-tls.co.uk/articles/front-house-british-museum. Accessed 17 January 2021.

Benedictus, L. (2015) Hajj Crush: How Crowd Disasters Happen and How They Can be Avoided, *The Guardian*, www.theguardian.com/world/2015/oct/03/hajj-crush-how-crowd-disasters-happen-and-how-they-can-be-avoided. Accessed 3 May 2021.

Brilliant Idea Studio (2022) The Importance of a Visitor Experience Strategy, https://brilliantideastudio.com/museums/the-importance-of-visitor-experience-strategy. Accessed 21 April 2022.

Burch, A. (2013) *Audience Advocacy: a Visitor-Centred Approach*, www.culturehive.co.uk/wp-content/uploads/2013/07/Audience-advocacy-a-visitor-centred-approach..Alex-Burch..2005.pdf. Accessed 17 January 2021.

Burton, O. (2021) Interview conducted by the author, 6 May 2021.

Charr, M. (2019) Museums and Employee Diversity, *Museum Next*, www.museumnext.com/article/museums-and-employee-diversity. Accessed 1 December 2021.

Chen, C. (2012) Representing and Interpreting Traumatic History: a Study of Visitor Comment Books at the Hiroshima Peace Memorial Museum, *Museum Management and Curatorship*, **27**, 375–92.

Collins Dictionary (2021) Duty Manager, definition, www.collinsdictionary.com/dictionary/english/duty-manager.

Conn, D. (2019) 30 Years of Seeking Justice: Hillsborough Disaster Timeline, *The Guardian*, www.theguardian.com/football/2017/jun/28/long-road-justice-hillsborough-inquest-timeline. Accessed 3 May 2021.

Devereaux, M. (2021) Interview conducted by author, 13 June 2021.

DHT (Dundee Heritage Trust) (2022) Verdant Works Story, www.verdantworks.co.uk/verdant-works-story. Accessed 4 January 2022.

Dingsøyr, T., Nerur, S., Balijepally, V. and Brede Moe, N. (2012) A Decade of Agile Methodologies: Towards Explaining Agile Software Development, *Journal of Systems and Software*, doi: 10.1016/j.jss2012.02.033.

Donoghue, B. (2019) *Presentation for Visit East of England*, ALVA, www.visiteastofengland.com/wp-content/uploads/2019/08/Bernard-Donoghue-ALVA.pdf. Accessed 13 June 2022.

Doran, G. T. (1981) There's a S.M.A.R.T. Way to Write Management's Goals and Objectives, *Management Review*, **70** (11), 35–6.

Egan, M. E. (2015) Fostering Innovation Through a Diverse Workforce, *Forbes Insights*, https://images.forbes.com/forbesinsights/StudyPDFs/Innovation_Through_Diversity.pdf. Accessed 1 February 2022.

EH (English Heritage) (2019) *On-Site Visitor Experience Strategy 2019–2023.*

Eid, H. (2018) Connecting the Dots: The Impact of Diversity in the Museum Workforce on Innovation, Relevance and Audience Engagement. In the *2018 Museums and the Web Conference Proceedings (Vancouver, Canada)* and online: https://mw18.mwconf.org/paper/connecting-the-dots-the-impact-of-diversity-in-the-museum-workforce- on-innovation-relevance-and-audience-engagement.

Falk, J. H. (2009) *Identity and the Museum Visitor Experience,* Left Coast Press.

Falk, J. H. (2016) Museum Audiences: A Visitor-Centred Perspective, *Loisir et Société/Leisure and Society,* **39** (3), 357–70.

Falk, J. H. and Dierking, L. D. (2016) *The Museum Experience Revisited,* Routledge.

Feldman, K. (2020) Guidance and Gratitude: On Cultural Leadership in Uncertain Times, *Apollo Magazine,* www.apollo-magazine.com/kaywin-feldman-cultural-leadership-during-coronavirus-crisis. Accessed 3 April 2020.

Ferraro, J. and Henderson, J. (2011) Identifying Features of Effective Emergency Response Plans, *Journal of American Institute for Conservation,* **50**, 35–48.

Fiddler, A. (2022) Interview conducted by author, 21 January 2022.

FMJ (Fair Museum Jobs) (2021a) About Us, https://fairmuseumjobs.org/about-us. Accessed 1 December 2021.

FMJ (Fair Museum Jobs) (2021b) The Manifesto, https://fairmuseumjobs.org/manifesto. Accessed 1 December 2021.

FOH Museums (2019) *FOH Museums Research,* https://fohmuseums.wordpress.com/category/fohmuseums-research. Accessed 1 December 2021.

FOH Museums (2020) What are the Opportunities for Career Progression for FOH?, https://fohmuseums.wordpress.com/2020/12/01/what-are-the-opportunities-for-career-progression-for-foh. Accessed 10 April 2022.

Gammon, B. and Graham, J. (1998) Putting Value Back into Evaluation, *Visitor Studies Today,* **1,** (6), 6–8.

Gillett, L. (2016) *Customer Care Training Plan,* London Museum Development Volunteer Training Bank, www.museumoflondon.org.uk/application/files/1414/6486/9469/customer-care-training-plan.pdf. Accessed 6 November 2021.

Griffiths, P. (2021) Interview conducted by author, 12 January 2021.

Haley Goldman, K. (2022) Discover the Three Types of Museum Evaluation, *Dexibit,* https://dexib022it.com/the-three-types-of-museum-evaluation. Accessed 7 January 2022.

Haywood, N. (2018) Accompanied Visits as a Tool to Understand Visitors' Experiences: A Critical Reflection and Proposed Typology, *Visitor Studies,* **21**, 135–47.

Henderson, T. (2017) Why Innovation is Crucial to Your Organisation's Long-Term Success, *Forbes,* www.forbes.com/sites/forbescoachescouncil/2017/05/08/why-innovation-is-crucial-to-your-organizations-long-term-success/?sh=5c8c2e153098. Accessed 25 February 2022.

Hermon, E. (2022) Interview conducted by author, 6 August 2022.

Hingley, D. (2022) E-mail exchange with author, 11 April 2022.

Hope-Hailey, V. and Balogun, J. (2002) Devising Context Sensitive Approaches to Change: The Example of Glaxo Wellcome, *Long Range Planning*, **35** (2), 133–78.

Hough, A. (2008) Men Scouted Targets for 7/7 Bombings, *Reuters*, www.reuters.com/article/uk-britain-july7/men-scouted-targets-for-7-7-bombings-idUKL0845526520080410?edition-redirect=uk. Accessed 14 February 2021.

HRP (Historic Royal Palaces) (2020) George III: The Mind Behind the Myth, *Kew Palace*, www.hrp.org.uk/kew-palace/george-iii-the-mind-behind-the-myth/#gs.sf4r0z. Accessed 5 February 2021.

HRP (Historic Royal Palaces) (2022) About Us, www.hrp.org.uk/about-us/#gs.yyg5zy. Accessed 29 April 2022.

Huang, S., Weiler, B. and Assaker, G. (2014) Effects of Interpretive Guiding Outcomes on Tourist Satisfaction and Behavioural Intention, *Journal of Travel Research*, **54**, 344–58.

Hunwick-Brown, W. (2021) *Getting Down with the Kids*, Heritage Volunteering Group Case Studies, http://heritagevolunteeringgroup.org.uk/wp-content/uploads/2019/07/Youth-Volunteering-1.pdf. Accessed 6 December 2021.

HVG (Heritage Volunteering Group) (2021) *Creating Capacity 2021: Rebuilding Volunteering in the Heritage Sector Post Covid*, http://heritagevolunteeringgroup.org.uk/wp-content/uploads/2021/06/Creating-Capacity-Final-2021.pdf. Accessed 6 December 2021.

Jugg, S. (2022) E-mail exchange with C. Straughan, J. Allen, Rachel Mackay, 21 July 2022.

Kaplan, K. (2016) When and How to Create Customer Journey Maps, *Nielson Norman Group*, www.nngroup.com/articles/customer-journey-mapping. Accessed 20 February 2021.

Kime, N. (2020) Introduction to Ticketing for Museums and Galleries, *Museums Association*, www.museumsassociation.org/museums-journal/in-practice/2020/08/introduction-to-ticketing-for-museums-and-galleries. Accessed 3 May 2021.

Kotter, J. P. (1996) *Leading Change*, Harvard Business Review Press, Boston, MA.

Kübler-Ross Foundation (2023) Kübler-Ross Change Curve, www.ekrfoundation.org/5-stages-of-grief/change-curve. Accessed 10 April 2023.

Lane, C. (2022) E-mail exchange with author, 24 April 2022.

Lee, H.R. (2022) Multiple Generations: Perceptions and Problems, *The Intergenerational Expert*, www.intergenerationalexpert.com/multiple-generations-perceptions-problems. Accessed 13 June 2022.

Lewin, K. (1947) Frontiers in Group Dynamics: Concept, Method and Reality in Social Science, Social Equilibria and Social Change, *Human Relations*, **1** (5).

Lila Wallace – Reader's Digest Fund (2000) *Service to People: Challenges and Rewards. How Museums can Become More Visitor-Centred,* www.wallacefoundation.org/knowledge-center/Documents/How-Museums-Can-Become-Visitor-Centered.pdf. Accessed 19 February 2023.

Livescault, J. (2022) 16 Techniques to Encourage Innovation in the Workplace, *Braineet,* www.braineet.com/blog/encouraging-workplace-innovation. Accessed 25 February 2022.

MA (Museums Association) (2016) Valuing Diversity, www.museumsassociation.org/campaigns/workforce/inclusion/valuing-diversity. Accessed 24 November 2021.

MA (Museums Association) (2017) Guidelines to Address Low Sector Pay, www.museumsassociation.org/campaigns/workforce/pay-in-museums/#. Accessed 24 November 2021.

MA (Museums Association) (2022) *Salary Research and Recommendations,* www.museumsassociation.org/app/uploads/2022/11/MA-Salary-Research-and-Recommendations-2022.pdf. Accessed 19 February 2022.

Mackay, R. (2020a) Conflict Resolution, *The Recovery Room,* www.therecoveryroomblog.com/conflict-resolution. Accessed 3 September 2021.

Mackay, R. (2020b) The Shutdown Survey, *The Recovery Room,* www.therecoveryroomblog.com/blog/shutdown-survey. Accessed 7 December 2020.

Mackay, R. (2020c) Taking the Lead, *The Recovery Room,* www.therecoveryroomblog.com/taking-the-lead. Accessed 28 November 2020.

Mackay, R. (2021) No, Museums Should Not be 'Gloriously Empty', *Blooloop,* https://blooloop.com/museum/opinion/museum-visitors-return. Accessed 3 May 2021.

MacLeod, D. and Clarke, N. (2009a) *Engage for Success: Enhancing Performance Through Employee Engagement,* Engage for Success, https://engageforsuccess.org/wpcontent/uploads/2021/02/Engaging-for-Success.pdf. Accessed 10 April 2022.

MacLeod, D. and Clarke, N. (2009b) The Four Enablers, *Engage for Success,* https://engageforsuccess.org/the-four-enablers. Accessed 10 April 2022.

MacLeod, D. and Clarke, N. (2014) *The Evidence: Wellbeing and Employee Engagement,* Engage for Success, https://engageforsuccess.org/wp-content/uploads/2021/01/wellbeing-and-engagement-04June2014-Final.pdf. Accessed 10 April 2022.

McLellan, A. and Douglas, O. (2004) Objects Talk: Interpreting Objects Through Community Groups, *Journal of Museum Ethnography,* **16**, 56–63.

McMahon, K. (2021) Interview conducted by author, 26 November 2021.

Merriam-Webster (2022) Innovation, www.merriam-webster.com/dictionary/innovation?utm_campaign=sd&utm_medium=serp&utm_source=jsonld. Accessed 27 February 2022.

Merriman, N. (2000) *Beyond the Glass Case: The Past, the Heritage and the Public,* Leicester University Press.

MGS (Museums Galleries Scotland) (2021) *Skills for the Future,* www.museumsgalleriesscotland.org.uk/projects/skills-for-success-legacy. Accessed 24 November 2021.

MGS (Museums Galleries Scotland) (2022) Understanding Your Audiences Through Evaluation, www.museumsgalleriesscotland.org.uk/advice/evaluation/understanding-your-audiences-through-evaluation. Accessed 7 January 2022.

MHM (Morris Hargreaves McIntyre) (2021) Culture Segments, https://mhminsight.com/culture-segments. Accessed 6 November 2021.

Mitroff Silvers, D. (2016) Design Sprints for Visitor Experience Advocacy: 5 Lessons from the British Museum, *Design Thinking for Museums,* https://designthinkingformuseums.net/2016/08/26/design-sprints-british-museum. Accessed 16 January 2022.

Morioka, E. (2021) Interview conducted by author, 21 December 2021.

Morrison, S. (2022) Interview conducted by author, 12 May 2022.

NCVO (National Council for Voluntary Organisations) (2021a) Keeping Volunteers, https://beta.ncvo.org.uk/help-and-guidance/involving-volunteers/supporting-and-managing-volunteers/keeping-volunteers. Accessed 6 December 2021.

NCVO (National Council for Voluntary Organisations) (2021b) Solving Volunteer Problems, https://beta.ncvo.org.uk/help-and-guidance/involving-volunteers/supporting-and-managing-volunteers/solving-volunteer-problems. Accessed 6 December 2021.

NCVO (National Council for Voluntary Organisations) (2021c) Training Volunteers, https://beta.ncvo.org.uk/help-and-guidance/involving-volunteers/valuing-and-developing-volunteers/training-volunteers. Accessed 6 December 2021.

NCVO (National Council for Voluntary Organisations) (2021d) Writing a Volunteer Agreement, https://beta.ncvo.org.uk/help-and-guidance/involving-volunteers/recruiting-and-welcoming-volunteers/writing-a-volunteer-agreement. Accessed 6 December 2021.

NCVO (National Council for Voluntary Organisations) (2021e) Writing a Volunteer Strategy, https://beta.ncvo.org.uk/help-and-guidance/involving-volunteers/understanding-volunteering/why-involve-volunteers. Accessed 6 December 2021.

NCVO (National Council for Voluntary Organisations) (2021f) Why Involve Volunteers? https://beta.ncvo.org.uk/help-and-guidance/involving-volunteers/understanding-volunteering/why-involve-volunteers. Accessed 6 December 2021.

Oakley, M. (2021) Interview conducted by the author, 6 December 2021.

Paqua, M. and Stewart, S. (2018) Visitor Journey Mapping in Museums, *Pratt Institute,* https://museumsdigitalculture.prattsi.org/visitor-journey-mapping-in-museums-f18442ee1d99. Accessed 20 February 2021.

Parsons, E. (2020) Understanding Your Audiences, *Association of Independent Museums,* www.aim-museums.co.uk/wp-content/uploads/2020/04/Understanding-Your-Audiences-2020-1.pdf www.emmaparsonsconsulting.com. Accessed 7 January 2022.

Pearson, C. (2017) *Museums in the Second World War: Curators, Culture and Change,* Routledge.

Philips, P. A. (2019) Using Customer Journey Maps to Enrich Your Museum Visitor Experience, *Association of Independent Museums,* www.aim-museums.co.uk/using-customer-journey-maps-enrich-museum-visitor-experience. Accessed 20 February 2021.

Power, L. (2021) E-mail exchange with author, 10 December 2021.

Protect UK (2022) Bomb Threats, Protect UK, www.protectuk.police.uk/incident-procedures. Accessed 10 April 2023.

Q-LINE Consulting (2022) The Stained-Glass Museum, www.qlineconsulting.com/case-studies/stained-glass-museum. Accessed 20 July 2022.

Renaissance East of England (2008) *Evaluation Toolkit for Museum Practitioners,* http://visitors.org.uk/wp-content/uploads/2014/08/ShareSE_Evaltoolkit.pdf. Accessed 10 April 2021.

Rodliff, J. (2022) Interview conducted by author, 30 April 2022.

Schmidt, C. (1979) Guided Tours: Insulated Adventure, *Urban Life,* **7**, 441–67.

Sharma, M. (2022) Top Tips: Successful Evaluation Planning, *The Audience Agency,* www.theaudienceagency.org/resources/top-tips-for-successful-evaluation-planning. Accessed 7 January 2021.

Shaw, A. (2020) More Than 40 British Museums and Conservators Donate Personal Protective Equipment to Help the NHS Fight the Covid 19 Crisis, *The Art Newspaper,* www.theartnewspaper.com/news/more-than-40-british-museums-and-conservators-donate-personal-protective-equipment-to-help-the-nhs-fight-the-covid-19-crisis. Accessed 5 August 2020.

Smith, L. and Campbell, G. (2015) The Elephant in the Room: Heritage, Affect and Emotion. In Logan W., Craith, M. and Kockel, U. (eds) *A Companion to Heritage Studies,* Wiley-Blackwell.

Stouten, J., Rousseau, D. M. and De Cremer, D. (2018) Successful Organisational Change: Integrating the Management Practice and Scholarly Literatures, *Academy of Management Annals,* **12** (2), 752–88.

Straughan, C. (2021) Maximise Your Income Generation, *Simon Spencer Associates,* www.stephenspencerassociates.com/blog/2021/04/19/maximise-your-income-generation-with-carly-straughan-2f4r4. Accessed 3 May 2021.

Taylor, T. C. (2021) Inclusive Hiring Practices Your Organisation Should Implement, *Academy to Innovate HR*, www.aihr.com/blog/inclusive-hiring. Accessed 1 December 2021.

Thackray Museum of Medicine (2022) *Business Plan 2022–23*, https://thackraymuseum.co.uk/wp-content/uploads/2022/01/TMM_Business_Plan_Digital_2022_23.pdf. Accessed 19 February 2023.

The Whole Story (2019) Tate: Time for Change, www.thewholestory.org.uk/connect-and-engage-stories/tate. Accessed 20 June 2023.

Trip Advisor (2021a) A Bad Experience was Handled Beautifully by the English Heritage Team, Stonehenge, www.tripadvisor.co.uk/ShowUserReviews-g528762-d188527-r794227461-Stonehenge-Amesbury_Wiltshire_England.html. Accessed 20 July 2022.

Trip Advisor (2021b) About Us, https://tripadvisor.mediaroom.com/uk-about-us. Accessed 16 April 2021.

Trip Advisor (2021c) Hidden London Review, www.tripadvisor.co.uk/Attraction_Review-g186338-d19590430-Reviews-Hidden_London-London_England.html. Accessed 6 May 2021.

UK Government (2016) Disability Confident Employers, https://disabilityconfident.campaign.gov.uk. Accessed 10 April 2023.

UK Government (2019) Agency Workers Regulations 2010: Guidance for Recruiters, www.gov.uk/government/publications/agency-workers-regulations-2010-guidance-for-recruiters. Accessed 1 December 2021.

Vagnone, F. D. and Ryan, D. E. (2016) *Anarchist's Guide to Historic House Museums*, Left Coast Press.

Wallace, V. (2013) *Success Guides: Successful Visitor Experience – Getting it Right*, Association of Independent Museums, www.aim-museums.co.uk/wp-content/uploads/2017/02/Successful-Visitor-Experience.pdf. Accessed 19 February 2023.

Weiler, B. and Black, R. (2015) *Tour Guiding Research: Insights, Issues and Implications*, Channel View Publications.

Williams, M. (2017) The Bullying and Fear at the Heart of Zero-Hour Contracts, *The Guardian*, www.theguardian.com/careers/2017/mar/27/the-bullying-and-fear-at-the-heart-of-zero-hour-contracts. Accessed 1 December 2021.

Young, J. (2020) Pre-Booking Insights for Visitor Attractions, *BVA BDRC*, www.bva-bdrc.com/opinions/pre-booking-insights-for-visitor-attractions. Accessed 3 May 2021.

Index